ACTING
THROUGH
EXERCISES

ACTING

THROUGH

EXERCISES

*A Synthesis of Classical and
Contemporary Approaches*

John L. Gronbeck-Tedesco
University of Kansas

Mayfield Publishing Company
Mountain View, California
London · Toronto

Library of Congress Cataloging-in-Publication Data

Gronbeck-Tedesco, John L.
    Acting through exercises : a synthesis of classical and contemporary approaches / John L. Gronbeck-Tedesco.
        p.   cm.
    Includes bibliographical references and index.
    ISBN 0–87484–947–0
    1. Acting.   I. Title.
PN2061.G747   1991
792'.028—dc20   91–12008
                                                                              CIP

Manufactured in the United States of America
10   9   8   7   6   5   4   3

Mayfield Publishing Company
1240 Villa Street
Mountain View, California 94041

Sponsoring editor, Lansing Hays; managing editor, Linda Toy; production editor, Sondra Glider; manuscript editor, Carol Dondrea; text and cover designer, Donna Davis; photographer, Tom Emmerich; production artist, Jean Mailander.

The text was set in 10/12 ITC Garamond Light by TBH/Typecast and printed on 50# Finch Opaque by Malloy Lithographing.

Page 132: Quotation from David Mamet, *Sexual Perversity in Chicago*, ©1971, 1977 reprinted by permission of the author. Page 132: Quotation from Brian Friel, *Lovers*, © 1968 by Brian Friel, reprinted by permission of International Creative Management, Inc. Part opener photos courtesy of University of Kansas Photographic Services.

To my extended family: Fred, Lucy, and Rick, Tom and Jo, Joe and Josephine, Mary, Sara, and Pat; and to my spouse and children: Susan, Anna, and John.

Unless the eye catch fire
The God will not be seen
Unless the ear catch fire
The God will not be named
Unless the heart catch fire
The God will not be loved
Unless the mind catch fire
The God will not be known

William Blake

Where do I go from here? I'm not sure. . . .
I feel like I've been on a long journey and
now that I've reached my destination, I
realize I'm back at the beginning.

Mark Daniel Nash, *Acting from Stillness*

Brief Contents

Contents

Chapter 14: Body Strategies: Rigid, Dense, Collapsed, Swollen 231

Preface

Once upon a time, different versions of the System and the Method cornered the market on American actor training. But since the mid-sixties, new voices and ideas have gradually expanded the traditional training regimen. Grotowski, Schechner, Chaikin, Barba, Morowitz, Brook, Feldenkrais, and Alexander; bioenergetics, gestalt psychology, the human potential movement, object relations theory, neurolinguistic processing, yoga and the martial arts: All have contributed, directly and indirectly, to contemporary performance pedagogy. This is not to say that the old masters have been displaced. On the contrary, Stanislavski, Boleslavsky, Strasberg, Adler, Hagen, Lewis, Moore, Hull, Meisner, and others have become important in new ways. First, their approaches still provide some of the language and categories (and sometimes prejudices) used to organize training. Second, many of their basic exercises continue to be taught alongside those from more recent sources.

The upshot is that American acting is becoming a jubilantly eclectic affair in which new and old protocols are juxtaposed and mixed—but often unconsciously and with uneven results. This book comes largely out of a desire to integrate new and old. Its main purpose is to provide a practical synthesis of some of those divergent practices that are increasingly a part of mainstream actor education.

In fashioning this synthesis, I have tried to coordinate the assortment of protocols that teachers now have to choose from without sacrificing the benefits of pluralism. One part of my job has been to discover conceptual frameworks which bring together approaches that would otherwise appear inconsistent or remain disconnected from one another. Another part has been to modify some exercises so that they jibe with one another but do so without losing any of their power.

Because performance training is partially an oral tradition, the research for this book has taken a full ten years. Much of that research has consisted chiefly of talking to lots of people—or rather, getting them to talk to me, often in the context of workshops, courses, or lectures, but sometimes in casual conversations.

Since the project is to bring together approaches from different teaching communities, some attention to theory is inevitable. Now, theory is a lot like chocolate. Some people cannot get enough of it, and others do not understand what all the salivating is about. When is enough enough? Early on, I decided that this text would be useful in the studio. So, I have constrained my own taste for theory to some extent and summarized methodological notions rather than offer full discussions. But notice the hedge in "to some extent." Often, I have tried to provide conceptual frameworks for the exercises that invite students to reflect on both the significance of acting and their own involvement in it. A note I often give in class is that part of the actor's craft is to get beyond craft. Knowing and doing are part of one another.

RECURRING THEMES

A number of different themes appear and reappear throughout the book, changing with each new context, like the characters in a play. Before beginning, it might be useful to review some of these.

The Body

Energy is the only life and is from the Body; . . .
WILLIAM BLAKE

Throughout the text, I have viewed the body as the *active habitat* for all human experience. The ecological metaphor points out that the body is both the locus (the where) and the sponsor (the how) of all our experiences and therefore is always contributing to them in some way.

The implications of this view are rich. No longer is the body relegated only to the "outer" side of the inner/outer distinction (which has been one of the most powerful methodological divisions in American acting pedagogy). As the habitat for all human experience, the body is on both sides of the distinction at the same time. That is, it contributes to both inner and outer experience. This means that the body is not just an outer, *expressive* medium for the actor's inner life; it also performs an *im-pressive* role by helping to stimulate and shape that interior world of associations, memories, impulses, and feelings.

The traditional expressive role of the body in acting is summarized by Jack Clay:

[T]hose of us who were students of Strasberg . . . sooner or later found ourselves facing . . . fundamental problems. These dealt with what is usually called voice and body work. The fact is, in our basic "method" training, which is essentially education in responding, it was not always possible to get the actor to react openly, freely, and expressively to imaginary stimuli. Blocking the way for many actors were the eccentricities of their own habitual behavior, movement, and speech.

"Self-Use in Actor Training," *TDR,* 16:1 (March 1972), p. 16

Clay captures the typical legitimation for body and voice training: to make possible the physical (outer) expression of the actor's psychological (inner) states. Stanley Keleman clarifies the im-pressive role from the perspective of bioenergetics:

All sensations, all emotions, all thoughts are, in fact, organized patterns of motion.

[and]

Feelings are the result of cellular pulsations, metabolism, cytoplasmic currents, . . . [physical] motility.

Embodying Experience, pp. 3, 34

He helps us grasp how the body participates in states that we may sense as inner, psychological, emotional, or even spiritual.

I have treated the body as both—as a contributor to both inner and outer experience and as both expressive and im-pressive. I hope the exercises will make students aware of just how deeply and ubiquitously the body participates in all the processes of living and acting.* The fact that the body plays a part in all varieties of human experience does not mean that terms like *internal* and *external, emotional* and *somatic, psychological* and *physical* are abolished. Their role is considerably revised, however. Instead of telling us where our experiences take place, they help to describe how experiences feel. The shift is from ontology to phenomenology. These words help us focus on whatever aspect of experience we are most in touch with at a particular moment.

Integration

The concept of the body as active in the construction of all experience actually helps the integration of newer and older approaches, mentioned earlier.

A major strategy used in constructing exercises has been to combine work that once was separated according to the traditional inner and outer divisions. For example, in the first three chapters, movement and breathing

---

*Thanks to Meyerhold, Vakhtangov, Michael Chekhov, Copeau, St. Denis, Dalcroze, Grotowski, Cynkutis, Schechner, and Chaikin, who set the stage for these thoughts about the actor's body.

are often connected to work with images, associations, and impulses. And the psychological states of security, openness, and stillness are associated directly with physical protocols. Similarly, in Chapter 5, there are exercises that join materials from object relations theory, traditional affective memory, and bioenergetics. In Chapter 6, some of the exercises combine sense memory (à la Strasberg) with sound and motion work (derived in part from Grotowski).

For the most part, the exercises are gentle and straightforward. Connecting inner and outer work is done simply and in stages. I have preferred to present sequences of exercises that build on one another rather than providing one or two exercises that attempt to accomplish too much.

Culture

Actors are situated. They both live and participate in their culture. Where training is concerned, culture is a force to be reckoned with. Not all of the conditioning students receive from their world contributes positively to their work in the theatre. Some of the most fundamental skills presented in this book begin the process of unlearning certain habits while trying to establish others that are more useful on stage.

Confronting some of the issues of culture and conditioning helps to avoid confusion. Many students quickly become sensitive to the incongruity between the life-habits they have already acquired and the acting skills they are trying to learn. Talking about some of these incongruities reduces puzzlement and the potential for anxiety when the demands of socialization conflict with those of performance training.

Re-forming habits is not a simple matter. Nineteen or more years of socialization do not submit easily to a few exercises. Training is a lifelong undertaking. This book attempts to provide a few resources for the journey.

Others

The world outside the actor's skin is an important source of stimulation. Without excitation from the surroundings, there can be no such thing as experience. And although experiences might be subjective events, they nonetheless depend on our give-and-take with what lies beyond us.

Other actors are often the most important elements in that world outside the self. Some acting programs have begun to make much more of working with others than did the Method studios of the fifties and sixties, which tended to emphasize work on the "me."

The current focus on the actor's outward orientation is really a renascence, for it too has a history. For example, writing of Vakhtangov's contribution to contemporary training, William Kuhlke has noted:

The improvisational nature of their [Vakhtangov's company] work demanded certain things of them: First, they had to be acutely aware of their partners *as partners* (whatever characters they were playing) and adapt themselves to the . . . partner's work. . . . Only in that way could they generate and maintain the mutually re-enforcing creative energy that kept the work flowing.

"The Unclaimed Legacy of *Turandot*," pp. 7–8

And, although none of his translated works really emphasized working with others, Stanislavski himself wrote with reverence about "communion" and "ensemble." Even after the Method, with its inward focus, became the centerpiece of American training, there remained a few mainstream teachers, such as Sanford Mcisncr, who placed clear focus on the connective work between actors.

Some of the exercises in this text can be done alone, but the vast majority require the willing participation of a partner. Accordingly, I have placed a great deal of emphasis on professional courtesy and trust.

Transferring Skills to a Playscript

One of the perennial problems in performance training is helping students transfer what they learn in exercises to their work on scripted material. I have dealt with this issue fairly directly by including dialogue in several of the exercises, especially in Parts II, III, and IV. Sometimes students are asked to shuttle back and forth between verbal and nonverbal work. In other cases, words are mixed into an exercise gradually. The appendix provides short pieces of dialogue called jumps, as well as longer scenes. Jumps are very short texts that are general enough to be played by anyone, male or female. Their brevity (four to ten sentences divided between two actors) makes memorization simple and allows students to switch partners whenever necessary. The jumps and the scenes allow for both naturalistic and more stylized forms of work.

Empowerment

Many of the exercises, especially those in Parts II and III, are really strategies of empowerment. The goal of these exercises is to enable an actor to empower the people, things, and settings on stage to elicit responses from him or her. Properly understood, the notion of empowerment also applies to the more traditional mnemonic exercises such as sensory recall and affective memory. The actor works with the past so that its capacity to evoke feelings can be transferred and attached to people, places, and things of the present. Ultimately, the aim of empowerment is to make the actor more responsive to the world on stage by making that world more potent.

[W]hy does the training of actors seem to disregard the key ingredient of human survival and development— the soul? Why do we describe acting in "spiritual" terms and then teach acting as an acquired skill? . . . What could be more important than for a teacher of acting to help an actor rediscover his or her soul? . . .

WILLIAM J. DOAN, "BEYOND TECHNIQUE," IN *AMERICAN THEATRE*, NOVEMBER 1989, p. 7

Spirituality

Learning to act is more than merely acquiring a set of technical skills. It is a spiritual endeavor. No matter how troublesome such a notion may be, to ignore it is irresponsible. I believe that the sense of the spiritual does not come directly from any one set of exercises or explanations. Rather, it is a by-product of working on the craft. In a profession where the actor and acting so quickly become only commodities, however, it is easy to ignore (or even contemn) the spiritual awarenesses evoked by the daily work in the studio. Moreover, insofar as our language habits are in some measure the product of late industrial empiricism, it is all the more difficult to address spiritual sensibilities. Yet, to ignore the spiritual dimensions of the actor's experience is to ask our students to disown part of themselves. If we are to maintain our own integrity as teachers, we must acknowledge that the work in the studio can be spiritually heuristic.

USES OF THE BOOK

In America, acting programs vary widely in philosophy, faculty specialties, course progression, and student population. I have tried to write a text that affords teachers and students a lot of flexibility, and that could be used in more than one course from the beginning through the intermediate levels.

The progression in each chapter is from easier to slightly more difficult exercises. There are more exercises than most teachers could use even over two or three courses. This gives instructors the opportunity to choose some for use in class and to assign others as homework. The number of exercises also allows teachers to individualize the training somewhat, so that different exercises addressing the same principle can be chosen with the needs of particular students in mind. (Individuating the exercise assignments is a particularly useful homework strategy.) Simply reading the exercises is also useful, not only as a way of clarifying principles but also because, as Feldenkrais and others have pointed out, reading can stimulate the imagination in a way that yields some of the same impact as actually doing the work.

The abundance of exercise material also allows the book to be divided up in a number of ways. Certain chapters can be taught in one course, while others can be reserved for another. Or, in those programs where a very few courses have to cover a lot of ground, teachers can use the first one or two subsections from several or all of the chapters. A variation on this same idea is to teach most of the subsections in each chapter, but limit the number of exercises used during class to accommodate time constraints.

The exercises are also etudes. That is, they open up avenues of exploration that can lead your students in directions not anticipated by the instructions and explanations I have provided. Each chapter has some blank pages at the end where your students can keep a journal to help them get at their own individual reactions to the work and to keep an ongoing record of your commentary. (I say more about keeping a journal in the "Introduction.") Good texts—whether in theatre or some other field—always seem to invite spontaneous "rewriting," because they provoke human growth, which is always, to some extent, unpredictable. Sometimes the best journeys are the ones we did not intend to take.

But while *Acting Through Exercises* is accommodating on some counts, it cannot meet all needs. It is not teacher-proof. Like texts in calculus, sociology, or French, this one assumes not only that you understand the subject but that you pursue it as a major interest. No textbook is a substitute for a good teacher.

Besides interest and dedication, *Acting Through Exercises* makes one more demand—namely, a devotion to the liberal arts as the basis for understanding acting. The libraries of Stanislavski, Strasberg, Elia Kazan, Meyerhold, and Grotowski are a testament to the breadth of learning it takes to be a great theatre artist or teacher. One of the missions of this book is to promote a desire for learning in those who would become actors. Psychology, philosophy, sociology, anthropology, history, physiology, biology, and so on all provide the assumptions and principles on which the actor's craft is grounded. Rather than skirt this simple truth, I have tried to celebrate it. The explanations and training strategies presented in the text lead to and from the liberal arts. They are the source of its energy and panache.

ACKNOWLEDGMENTS

Many have influenced this book. Some have been my teachers for long periods of time; others have led workshops that I was privileged to attend. Still others have shared their insights in more informal ways—across cups of coffee, in the hallways outside lecture halls, in greenrooms, or shoulder to shoulder at parties after a show. Many have careers in the theatre or film. But some have shed new light on acting and performance from the perspective of other disciplines. My thanks to all who spent time with me: Robert Altman, Marge Barstow, Joe and Jan Bonano, Sam Becker, Willard Bellman, Robert Benedetti, David Bergeron, Helen Backlin, James Brock, Paul Campbell, Maryellen Clemons, Jeff Corey, Zbigniew Cynkutis, Jed Davis, Walter Eysselink, Heinrick Falk, Robert Findlay, Earl Gister, Lewin Goff, Patrick Gouran, Bruce Gronbeck, Roger Gross, Marsha Grund, Ernie Guderjahn, Mary Sigsund-Guderjahn, George Gunkle, Moses Gunn, Chez Haehl, William Haushalter, Paul Kaufman, Jerome Kilty, Jeanne Klein, David Knauf, Kevin Kuhlke, Arthur Lessac, William Marshall, Bernard McCormick, Charles Neuringer, Donovan Ochs, Jack Oruch, Louis B.

Palter, James Peterson, Glenn Pierce, Delores Ramsey, Mark Reaney, Delores Ringer, Bari Rolf, Wilberto Rosario, David Schaal, Richard Schechner, Andrew Tsubaki, Delbert Unruh, William Valle, Kennis Wessel, Ronald Willis, Donald Wilson, and Jack Wright.

Special thanks must go to William Kuhlke, Paul Meier, and Marsha Paludan, who commented on earlier versions of the manuscript, and to Beth Reiff for encouraging me to include certain exercises that otherwise would not have appeared.

I owe a particular debt to Lansing Hays who through this entire project was the finest of editors. To him, Karen Dunlap, Carol Dondrea, Sondra Glider, Debby Horowitz, and Pam Trainer, thank you. Also to be thanked are Dede Corvinus, University of North Carolina at Chapel Hill; Virginia Drake, West Valley College; Jerry S. Krasser, University of Connecticut; James Norwood, University of Minnesota; Dennis Smith, Southern Oregon State University; and James Wilson, University of Southern California, who commented so generously and honestly on earlier drafts.

I must acknowledge Carol Caputo, Diane DeArmond, Alan Lopez, Nancy Swafford, and Charles Sheridan who helped me understand bioenergetics and gestalt psychology from the inside. To the Menninger Clinic, my gratitude for the use of its wonderful library, as well as to Paul Pruyser and Glenn Gabbard, who suggested several helpful readings. But none of those mentioned are responsible for the various interpretations (and simplifications) of psychological material that appear in this text.

I thank George Woodyard, Frances Horowitz, Ted Wilson, Andrew Debiki, and Janet Riley of the University of Kansas for their generosity in supporting some of the research that has contributed to this volume.

For his technical expertise and good taste during the photography sessions, I thank Tom Emmerich. Thanks also to Keri Paludan, Jon Chiccolini, Marsha Paludan, and William Kuhlke for allowing themselves to be photographed. And, for their forgiveness throughout the project, thanks to the intrepid word processors: Lynn Porter, Marilyn Heath, Melissa Ryckert, Pam LeRow, and Paula Malone.

My acknowledgments would not be complete without a word about the exercises. When I know the source of an exercise, I mention it either in the main body of the text or in the notes or references at the end of the chapters. But there are several exercises whose sources I do not recall, probably because exercises tend to get passed around until they become part of the air we all breathe, however unconsciously. After fifteen years of teaching, I cannot always tell the difference between what is mine and what I have inherited from others. Of course, the versions of the exercises presented here are my own and those who influenced me are not responsible for my departures from their original intentions.

Introduction

Learning to act is a journey of a particular kind. In some journeys, we simply sit in a seat and wait to get to a destination. If the trip is a long one, we may fill up the time with a variety of activities: reading, solitaire, catching up on some much needed rest. Such journeys require little effort on our part. More important, they do little to change us. When we step off a taxi or leave an airplane, we seldom feel that there is anything new about us. We might have collected a few pieces of lint and our clothing may be a bit rumpled, but we usually have not undergone important changes.

There are other kinds of journeys though, far different from the sort that we normally take. Acting is one of these "other kinds." Learning to act is a journey of *personal formation*. Formative journeys are supposed to re-form the traveler, to make him or her a different sort of person. These journeys may have a specific destination, but they do not have a simple and direct route. Most often, they require lots of exploration, purposeful wandering, side trips where the way is not always clear.

A formative journey is far from passive. It requires the full participation of the sojourner—spontaneity and discipline, caution and abandon, intuition and thought, planning and improvisation. Formative journeys require putting together a number of human capacities we may have thought of as separate and opposite.

In these days of instant gratification, quick relief, easy excitement, and formulae for immediate success, there is often little attention and even less tolerance for the kind of journey you are about to undertake. I want to offer you just a few guidelines before you begin—notions that other students seem to have found useful.

You are so young, so before all beginning, and I want to beg you, as much as I can, to be patient toward all that is unsolved in your heart.

RAINER MARIA RILKE,
"LETTERS ON LOVE"

1

1. What kind of actor you become will depend directly on what you pick up on your journey. For example, a particular exercise is not just another hoop you have to jump through in order to "get to act." The exercises and ideas you encounter in this book or in the classroom are supposed to change you—your voice, your body, the way you feel and think—you.

2. Acting is not just a bunch of skills that do not touch you. The skills become part of you and the way you live.

3. Keep a journal. At the end of each chapter are several pages you can use to write down your reactions to the training. The journal will give you an opportunity to personalize the exercises by discussing whatever thoughts, feelings, or associations they might trigger. You can also use the blank pages to add exercises your teacher suggests or to create some of your own.

   It is a good idea to think about the impact your training is having on your life outside the classroom. For example, some students have found that over time the movement exercises improve their mood. Others have discovered an increase in the variety and intensity of the feelings, thoughts, associations, and memories they experience. If you should happen to get a part in a play, your journal will give you a place to jot some notes on whatever light the experience sheds on your training. Journal entries can also provide useful material for teacher–student conferences. But most important, they give you the opportunity to make all the work you do your own.

4. The journey and the destination are the same. Imagine yourself standing there, on the stage of an important theatre or a film studio. But when you are actually in that position, you won't be watching yourself. Both consciously and unconsciously, you will be using all the things you have learned about acting, because they will be part of you. In other words, you will still be traveling, even while you are in front of an audience or camera. For the experience of acting a part becomes another excursion, another contribution to your pilgrimage of professional and personal growth—that is, an experience that, if you treat it properly, will get inside you and teach you something.

Where acting is concerned, you are never "there." Or, you are always already "there." Both statements can be true because the only place to be—the place that is the actor's "there," the place that is his or her true destination—is not fixed or static. It is not a particular role or job or contract, but the journey itself.

Think of a tree. The leaves are like all the parts you dream of playing. But there can be no leaves without a trunk to support and nurture them. The trunk is the actor's journey of personal formation. No matter how twisted and circuitous it may become, the journey is the source of everything.

When we worry too much about results, we tend to forget that the results must come from somewhere.
WILLIAM KUHLKE

Everyday, you will get together and work with one another. And, by the way, *you will play Hamlet or other great parts. But it must be* by the way.
ZBIGNEW CYNKUTIS

Getting Ready to Act:
Security, Openness, and Stillness

Part I deals with security, openness, and stillness. Before beginning, though, it is important to understand why these preliminaries are so crucial to your training.

Athletes spend long hours in the gym doing exercises that look nothing like what they do on the court or field. A bench press does not resemble a pass. But most professional quarterbacks use a carefully designed weight program to improve their passing. Similarly, riding an exercise bike or running laps around a stadium does not look or feel like what a pitcher does on the mound. Yet big league pitchers spend long hours working on their leg muscles and respiratory endurance.

Looks are deceiving. The conditioning regimen of serious athletes is the foundation of their craft. *What is true of athletes is equally true of many artists. For instance, the exciting work of dancers and singers rests on a foundation of rigorous exercises that may look or sound little like the final product. But the conditioning actually creates the neurophysical structures that make great performances possible. The point here for actors is an important one: Although the exercises in Part I may not always resemble acting on stage, they are nonetheless crucial in the same way as the conditioning done by athletes and other artists.*

There is nothing wrong with doing some acting very early in your training, whether in the form of scene work or as part of full-fledged productions. But to do so without a concurrent program of basic conditioning makes no sense. A strong foundation will speed up your progress in acquiring other acting skills, increase the power of your expression, and broaden the range of roles you are able to play. Without proper conditioning, you may still be able to entertain an audience in a superficial way, but you will never have an impact on the deepest part of their humanity. The best acting changes people's lives.

Of course, there are some basic differences between an actor's fundamental conditioning and that of most athletes, dancers, and singers. While theirs is primarily physical, yours combines work that is explicitly physical, emotional, psychological, and spiritual. Moreover, an actor's conditioning program also develops spontaneity, stimulates imagination, and heightens responsiveness.

Athletes, dancers, and singers never outgrow their need for the basic conditioning that makes their crafts possible. Neither do actors. The exercises in Part I (or exercises like them) should become part of your daily life and accompany you throughout your career. As you work through the first three chapters, be on the lookout for exercises that you find particularly interesting and constructive. These will eventually form your personal daily warm-up. Thirty to forty-five minutes' worth of exercises should be enough. Include a good mix of vigorous and gentle exercises. Also combine some that come easily with those that you find more challenging. It is best to consult an instructor before finalizing your warm-up list.

A sound warm-up serves a number of purposes: (1) It continues the developmental processes begun in these first three chapters; (2) helps you create a sense of discipline and dedication to your craft; and (3) prepares you for scene work or a full performance. Every two or three months, review your warm-up, replacing with new exercises those that seem to have grown stale. There are enough exercises in Part I to help you put together a wide variety of warm-up routines. In time you will be able to make up your own exercises.

Security

A growing sense of personal security is indispensable in all the work an actor does both in performance and in day-to-day training. *By security, I mean a sense of self-trust and personal well-being that permits an actor to encounter with confidence and relish whatever is happening on stage or in the studio.*

A clearer idea of how significant personal security really is comes from considering its opposite. When we are insecure—whether on stage or in everyday life—we worry about ourselves and monitor our behavior. We watch and listen to ourselves, always trying to make sure that we look and sound "right," and we are always certain that we do not. Insecure actors are constantly trying to fix themselves. Instead of focusing on what is happening at the moment, they become hopelessly locked up in themselves in a way that cuts off the possibility of a full, energetic interaction with the people or things in the surrounding environment.

Security brings a completely different orientation, one that frees the actor to concentrate more on the ongoing process of give-and-take with others. The integrity and completeness of this moment-to-moment process of giving and getting is one of the several important goals of an actor's training and the final result to which personal security contributes.

I know of no simple formula that will produce instant security on stage. But there are ways to work toward it gradually. In this chapter, performance security is viewed as a by-product of proper grounding, balance, breathing, and alignment—skills that are learnable and therefore part of the craft of acting. To get the most out of each exercise, read all the instructions first. Then go through the exercise slowly until you get the hang of it.

When a person remains on guard, even when there is very little or nothing to guard against, he succeeds not only in keeping others away but also in keeping himself from finding out what he can do.
GERALD KUSHEL, *CENTERING*

EXERCISES

Grounding

Grounding is one of several approaches to developing a heightened sense of personal security. To be firmly grounded is to be solidly in touch with the surfaces on which we stand, sit, or lie. Feeling grounded means feeling supported by whatever structure is beneath us as though it were our own personal foundation, safety net, root system, power plant—pick an analogy that suits you.

Grounding may seem like a straightforward physical process, but it also has important emotional and social dimensions. Full, confident contact with our ground promotes the freedom to take risks not only in the way we use our bodies on stage but also in the way we make contact with others. When we are out of touch with our ground, we have no basis from which to reach out toward the world. We tend to view others either as moorings to be depended on and clung to or as threats with the power to displace us or throw us off balance.

Exercise 1–1: The Bow

1. Take off your shoes and work on a hard surface. (Mats won't work for this exercise.)
2. Place your feet about 12"–18" apart (just inside your shoulder line should be about right).
3. Point your toes in so your stance becomes *slightly* pigeon-toed.
4. Make a loose fist of each hand and put the fists just below your belt line and a little behind your hips.
5. Bend your knees slightly and shift your weight toward the balls of your feet (but don't come up on your toes).
6. Lean back, gently pushing your pelvis forward slightly with your fists.
7. Try to make a bow-shaped arch, with your head and heels roughly in line with one another.
8. Now, breathe deeply but gently. Pretend you are breathing down into your legs.
9. As you exhale, try to relax and "let go" of your leg and pelvis muscles *without* coming out of position.
10. After three or four breaths come back to a normal stance and concentrate on allowing your feet to make full, loose contact against the floor.[1]

While doing the exercise, you may feel the muscles in your legs vibrating. This is supposed to happen. Muscular vibration means the movement in one muscle group is being passed along to others up and down your

THE BOW, STEP 9.
Keeping your eyes open
when your head is back
will make it easier for you
to keep your balance.
Remember to exhale and
relax during this step.

legs. This is a sign your leg muscles are organizing so movement and sensation can be conducted instead of constricted. (If this doesn't happen immediately, don't worry. There is no need to force anything. Sooner or later the vibrations will come.)

Exercise 1–2: The Bend

1. Stand with your feet comfortably apart and in a slightly pigeon-toed position.
2. Bend your knees a little; then bend over at the waist so that your *head* and *arms* hang loosely, and your fingertips lightly touch the floor or come close.
3. Place your weight on the balls of your feet.
4. Relax by inhaling into your legs and letting your muscles go as you exhale.
5. Hold the position for three or four breaths and return to a normal stance.
6. As in the previous exercise, try to feel the full, relaxed contact of your feet against the floor.

Once again, vibrations in your legs indicate that your muscles are responding to the position your legs are in.

It is important to let your
head and neck hang
loosely over your feet.

Exercise 1–3: The Leg Twist

Do this exercise gently. If you have a back, leg, or neck injury, it is best not
to do the exercise until you have healed.

1. Lie on your back with your knees bent and the soles of your feet on the
   floor about 6″–8″ apart.
2. Raise your right leg into the air at about a 45° angle with the knee bent.
3. Inhale gently. Then exhale and straighten your leg slowly. Come as close
   as you can to extending it fully, but stop short of allowing the experience to become painful.
4. Repeat the movement with your left leg.
5. Now lift both legs in the air with the knees bent. Turn your toes toward
   one another as though pigeon-toed, and bend your feet back to make
   roughly a 90° angle with your ankle.
6. Slowly straighten both legs. Exhale, letting go of your leg muscles. Complete three or four breathing cycles, bending your knees as you inhale
   and straightening them as you exhale.
7. End by placing your feet back on the floor and imagining the weight
   from the rest of your body traveling down and over your knees, into
   your feet.

*The nature of any
tree begins at the
roots. The body
must adjust to the
foot.*

CARLO MAZZONE-CLEMENTI,
"COMMEDIA AND THE
ACTOR," *TDR* 18, no. 1.

Exercise 1–4: Integrating the Voice

1. Repeat the last three exercises, being careful to follow the instructions.
2. When you come to the exhalation step, allow the effort you are putting
   into the exercise to pull a sound out of you. It may be a grunt or a groan,
   an "oh" or an "ah." Don't try for anything special. The important thing
   is that the sound is created or produced by the body work.

THE LEG TWIST,
STEP 2 (left).

STEP 5 (right).

Balance

Another means of achieving a more vivid feeling of personal security on stage is by developing a sense of balance. Balance is part of the way we deal with the demands the earth makes on our bodies—demands we sum up with the word *gravity*. A person is on balance when his or her physical organization provides the greatest number of possibilities for movement in a particular situation. Someone who is off balance is restricted from moving advantageously.

Balance and security are closely related. When you feel insecure, you tend to guarantee your balance by locking your knees, stiffening your hips, tensing your feet, or shifting your weight from one leg to the other. Risky social situations (such as being before an audience) often produce a tension between wanting to hold your ground and the desire to escape: two contradictory muscular organizations that upset balance and inhibit movement, breathing, and free self-expression.

Balance is relative, which means that it is an ever-shifting adjustment we make to our immediate circumstances. For example, the adjustments that keep an all-pro linebacker right-side up on the playing field might also make him a menace in the living room during a family argument. The social situation and our own emotional set-ups have an enormous influence on the way we respond to the gravity of a moment. An actor must be able to find his or her balance (i.e., most advantageous relationship to gravity) in a variety of situations.

The assumption emerging from the last two paragraphs is that physical work has a psychological impact. Balance (and security) developed on the physical level "spreads" to the psychological realm. In the martial arts, especially Aikido, physical balance is viewed as a fundamental source of both emotional well-being and personal energy. To be "a well-balanced person," to live a "balanced life," and "balancing" all the activities of a busy schedule may be more than metaphors and point ultimately to the way that physical, emotional, and social balance are related.

MOTION AND
BALANCE,
STEP 3 (left).
Use small hip circles that
allow you to comfortably
keep your balance.

STEP 4 (right).
Increase the size of the
circles gradually.

Exercise 1–5: Motion and Balance

Note: For the sake of safety, you may want to do this and the rest of the balance exercises on a mat.

1. Stand upright with your feet and heels together.
2. Extend your arms over your head and put your hands together as though in prayer. Relax without slumping.
3. Begin making small, relaxed circles with your hips.
4. Using your hands and arms as a counterbalance, allow the circles to grow in size and speed until you lose your balance (i.e., until you have to alter your stance to keep from falling).
5. Reground yourself by widening your stance, bringing your arms to your side, and loosening the muscles in your feet and lower legs, so that you make full, relaxed contact with the floor.

Guidelines: If you don't lose your balance, congratulations. Challenge yourself a bit more by doing the exercise on the balls of your feet.

Exercise 1–6: Balance from the Pyramid Position

1. Repeat the previous exercise.
2. This time begin with your feet at shoulder width so your hips and feet form a pyramid.
3. Try to discover where in your body you first feel the loss of balance. (Don't allow yourself to actually fall.)
4. Pay attention to the sensations in your feet, knees, pelvis, and back as you reground yourself.

Exercise 1–7: Incorporating the Voice

1. Do the previous exercise again but with your feet together.
2. Allow the hip circles to pull a sound from you.
3. Change the sound gradually until you find one that seems to make the physical movement freer and easier.
4. Notice whether or not the sound changes as you begin to lose your balance.
5. Reground yourself slowly and completely. The most important thing to remember is to let the *same effort* that creates the circles produce the sound. Avoid dividing your energy between sound and movement.

Exercise 1–8: Moving from Sound

1. Begin by making a sound—choose something simple that permits you to breathe normally.
2. Join the hip circles to the sound.
3. Discontinue the sound as soon as you feel your balance *begin* to go. Does stopping the sound seem to help you regain your balance, or does it disrupt your balance even more?

The voice is part of the body. Our culture teaches us to forget this and believe that voice is only an extension of intellect—that is, "the voice of reason" and that sort of thing. For an actor, the voice is not only a sense-making device but also a means for doing something to others: seducing, punishing, torturing, badgering, caressing, comforting, nurturing, and so on. A playwright may supply you with "all the right words." But it is up to you to give the words a physical presence that has an impact on those on stage and in the audience. When John Gielgud, Laurence Olivier, or Meryl Streep speak, their voices affect us deeply. They make us feel what they mean. But this cannot occur unless the voice is allowed a full, dynamic relationship with the rest of the actor's body.

Exercise 1–9: Sound and Balance: Voice

1. Repeat the last exercise.
2. Try to find a sound that actually helps you keep your balance beyond the point where you usually lose it.
3. Spend some time regrounding yourself.

Exercise 1–10: Backward Roll

1. Sit on a mat and clasp your knees to your chest, allowing your back to become round. (Be sure to work on a mat and be careful.)
2. Bend your head forward toward your knees, tucking your chin against your chest.
3. Concentrate on feeling the full weight of your buttocks against the floor. Relax by taking a deep breath and exhaling gently.
4. Take another breath and as you exhale *roll* backward onto your back. (If you find rolling backward scary, skip the exercise. Fear is a teacher, but a lousy one.)
5. Wait a moment; then let go of your legs and unfold, placing your knees up and the soles of your feet against the floor. Feel your back soften against the mat as you exhale.

Exercise 1–11: The Rocker

1. Take the same position as for the last exercise and roll onto your back. Keep your knees clasped to your chest and your chin down.
2. Pretend your back is a rocker and rock back and forth between the top of your buttocks and your shoulders.
3. Build up the rocking motion until it carries you over into a backward somersault. (It's best to make the somersault on your shoulder instead of your head.)

Guidelines: This should be a pleasurable experience. If it seems uncomfortable, don't complete the exercise.[2]

Breathing

> From our earliest moment of existence, we are molded and adjusted within a given social structure. All human greatness, servitude, and misery are the outcome of this adjustment. From the point of view of behavior, the social environment is the first and last important factor.
>
> Moshe Feldenkrais, *The Potent Self,* p. 30.

A forceful statement and a useful one for actors. Part of Feldenkrais's point is that even our fundamental physical processes are shaped by socialization. Breathing—one of the most basic and necessary forms of human behavior—is no exception.

All of you learned to breathe spontaneously, out of a need to survive. But the way you breathed as an infant changed as you grew up, in response to the "voices" in your social milieu. For example, some of you learned to breathe into your chests in order to make your stomachs look thin and flat. Or, you heard that breathing into your belly (so-called diaphragmatic breathing) somehow helps your voice sound better. You may never have been taught to appreciate the role of your back and sides in your day-to-day breathing activity. The problem is that the information we receive about breathing in the course of our daily lives is incomplete and usually goes unqualified. Socialization normally deals in general prescriptions and injunctions, with few if any "if's," "and's," or "but's." Moreover, socialization does not always teach what contributes to optimum human functioning; instead it imparts what others around you want to see and hear. An approach to breathing based solely on socialization may be enough to keep you alive, but it is probably not adequate to the demands of an acting career.

Over the years, many of you have acquired breathing habits that tend to overactivate certain parts of your torso and underactivate others. Such habits disturb balance and inhibit freedom of movement and personal expression. For instance, a person whose chest flairs and stomach disappears with every breath is quite literally a pushover, and someone whose chest sinks and belly swells is spending half of her or his life (half of each breathing cycle) with a torso shaped like an egg. Despite their nutritional value, eggs are not known for their ability to move freely and expressively.

In addition, breathing is not merely something that goes on along the front of the body. Muscles along the sides and back also contribute if allowed. In fact, for the next set of exercises, it is useful to think of breathing as a 360° activity. Stop reading for a moment and try to develop a sense of your torso (from your pelvis to your jaw line) as a cylinder that expands and contracts around its entire circumference and along its entire length.

The up-and-down movement of the cylinder may be slightly less distinct than the in-and-out, but both occur continuously. The ideal, of course, is to coordinate the action of the torso so that breathing is as free and complete as possible.

Breathing not only influences our balance and security, it is also central to a variety of vital processes. As the basis for respiration, breathing is the means by which we take in oxygen and transform it into usable energy. It is also the way we get rid of what's left of the air after the oxygen has been absorbed. Moreover, breathing is the source of our ability to make and sustain sound with our voices. A full and unforced breathing strategy is an important step toward a broader range of vocal capacities.

In addition, *our emotional lives are connected to the way we breathe.* Shallow breathing often helps us to minimize our feelings. Taking in less air, holding our breath, or exhaling quickly are ways of creating a mild paralysis that insulates us against our feelings. Freer, less erratic breathing has the opposite effect and prompts us toward a greater awareness of what we are feeling at the moment.

Many of the exercises in this section have been adapted from Moshe Feldenkrais, Frances Alexander, or their students. Breathe without straining for the results you think you are supposed to get. Be gentle with yourselves and take care.

Emotional freedom in the actor is directly related to correctly taken breath and is often the secret to a flood of appropriate feelings at the climax of a scene.

JACK CLAY, "SELF-USE IN ACTOR TRAINING," *TDR* 16, no. 1.

Exercise 1–12: Muscle Release

1. Lie on your back with your knees bent and your feet flat on the floor about 6"–10" apart.

2. Relax by "letting go" of your muscles as you exhale. Release your neck and shoulder muscles first, then your mid-back and chest, then your stomach and lower back, and finally your abdomen, buttocks, and upper thighs. *Take your time.* Do one muscle group at a time.

3. Concentrate on your back and focus on which parts make full contact with the floor and which do not. Repeat step 2 and see if there is any change.

Exercise 1–13: Chest Definition

1. Tighten your stomach muscles a little and breathe into your chest, allowing it to expand. As you exhale, allow your chest and stomach to relax.

2. Do this three or four times. As you inhale, pay special attention to what you feel (a) in your chest and upper back; (b) in your stomach and mid-back; (c) in your lower back and abdomen. As you exhale, release whatever tension you find in these muscle groups.

Exercise 1–14: Diaphragm Definition

1. This time leave your chest alone and pretend you are drawing air into your belly. As you inhale, let your muscles go so that your stomach expands.
2. As you exhale, let your loose stomach settle naturally as though it were deflating.
3. Repeat the exercise three or four times, paying attention to sensations in your chest, back, stomach, and pelvis. Once again, let go of tension.

Exercise 1–15: Full Torso Breathing

1. Begin by inhaling. But this time allow both your stomach and chest to expand. (Be careful not to hyperventilate by forcing in more air than you need.)
2. While exhaling, think of letting go of the muscles of your torso.
3. Complete the exercise according to the pattern given in the last two exercises, concentrating on undoing the tension in specific muscle groups of the torso and pelvis.

Exercise 1–16: Coordinating the Movements of the Torso

1. Remain on your back with your knees up and feet flat on the floor.
2. Tighten your stomach a little and inhale into your chest, allowing it to expand.
3. Hold your breath and imagine moving the air into your stomach so that your stomach expands and your chest deflates.
4. Relax and breathe normally.
5. Repeat the exercise four or five times.

Exercise 1–17: The Seesaw

1. In this exercise, it is important to use only as much effort as it takes *to enjoy* the muscular activity.
2. Breathe into your chest, keeping your stomach a bit taut.
3. Hold your breath and pass the air down and then up from your chest to your stomach and back again. Continue for as long as you can *comfortably* hold your breath.
4. Do this exercise three times, noticing movement in:
   a. your upper torso, front and back
   b. lower torso, especially the small of your back and lower stomach
   c. your pelvis, front and back

SEESAW AND ROCK,
STEP 2 (top).
The tilt of your head
need not be extreme.

STEP 3 (bottom).
Let your legs and hips
cooperate with the back-
and-forth movement of
your torso and head.

5. Now lie still and breathe normally (i.e., recall that it is a 360° activity), noticing whatever changes have occurred since you began this series of exercises.

Exercise 1–18: Seesaw and Rock

1. Repeat the last exercise.

2. As you gently push the air down to your stomach, allow the movement to pull your chin down slightly toward your chest.

3. As you move the air up, allow the motion to rock your head back a little so that your chin moves away from your chest.

4. This movement should include the pelvis, which will move in the same direction with your head.

5. Be gentle. A relaxed rocking motion is all that is necessary. Be sure to take a breath *before* you become uncomfortable.

6. Repeat the exercise three to five times; then lie still and observe changes in the way your breathing feels.

Exercise 1–19: Intercostal Definition

Intercostal muscles are located between the ribs and help the rib cage expand as you inhale. This exercise and the next will help to promote the more active participation of these muscles in your breathing.

INTERCOSTAL
DEFINITION, STEP 1
Get comfortable in this
position before going on.

1. Lie on your right side with your knees together and bent. Place your right arm along the floor and under your head so the right side of your face can rest on it. Get comfortable. For stability you might want to put your left palm down on the floor just in front of your chest.

2. Notice the way the right side of your rib cage meets the mat or floor.

3. Breathe naturally, allowing yourself to relax and loosen with each exhalation.

4. Now, breathe into your chest and concentrate on the sense of expansion along *both sides* of your rib cage. Repeat this section of the exercise three or four times.

5. Then breathe into your stomach, once again focusing on the sensations on both sides. Repeat this three or four times.

Exercise 1–20: Expanding the Movement of the Ribs I

1. Remaining on your side, reach your left hand up and clasp your right wrist.

2. Feel the greater expansion along your left side as you breathe normally.

3. Stay focused on your left side as you breathe first into your chest, then into your stomach.

4. Finish the exercise by breathing normally for three or four minutes.

Exercise 1–21: Expanding the Movement of the Ribs II

1. Turn onto your left side and repeat the last two exercises.

Exercise 1–22: Breathing into Your Back

1. Sit up with the soles of your feet together and your knees bent. The outsides of your feet should be on the floor.
2. Lean back and put most of your weight on your hands.
3. Let your head drop forward so your chin touches your chest. Loosen your neck muscles.
4. Round your back and shoulders comfortably. (This will happen automatically if your weight is on your hands.)
5. Tighten your stomach muscles a little. Instead of breathing into your chest, breathe into your upper back.
6. Concentrate on the sensations this creates in your back at the base of the neck and between the shoulder blades.
7. After three or four breaths, relax and breathe normally, holding the position for one or two more minutes.

Exercise 1–23: Finger Wrap with the Left Hand

1. Sit upright so your hands are off the floor. Put the soles of your feet together directly in front of you.
2. Round your back by placing your chin on your upper chest as in the last exercise.
3. Place the fingers of your left hand below and just behind your right armpit.
4. Breathe normally and feel the expansion under your fingers.
5. Now breathe two or three times into your upper back and the same number of times into your lower back.

BREATHING INTO
YOUR BACK, STEP 4.
The more you round
your back, the easier it
will be to feel it expand
when you breathe.

FINGER WRAP WITH
THE LEFT HAND,
STEP 3.

Exercise 1–24: Finger Wrap with the Right Hand

1. Keep the same position but with your right fingers behind and below your left armpit. Repeat the previous exercise.

Exercise 1–25: Synthesis

1. Lie on your back with your knees bent and the soles of your feet on the floor at a comfortable distance from one another.
2. Breathing normally, spend some time experiencing your torso as a cylinder that expands gently and easily in all directions.

Exercise 1–26: Breathing-Voice Association

1. Lie on your back with the soles of your feet on the floor at a comfortable distance from one another.

2. Breathing easily, make the following open vowel sounds in a normal voice:

a	(as in *cat*)	aw	(as in *law*)
ah	(as in *father*)	o	(as in *home*)
ahh	(as in *beyond*)	oo	(as in *fool*)

3. Make these sounds without overextending your lips or straining your jaw muscles. This is not a diction exercise.

4. Instead of listening to how your voice sounds, concentrate on how each sound feels in your body.

5. In order to avoid getting hooked on a particular sensation or sound, repeat the exercise using the middle, lower third, and upper third of your register.

Alignment

Alignment simply refers to the relationship among the structural components of the body, specifically between muscle groups and skeletal elements. Proper alignment in any situation is the physical organization that helps you achieve your specific goals. If you are trying to catch a ball, the best alignment is one that coordinates your movements and enables you to make the catch.

Roles often call for actors to pursue social or interpersonal goals, such as rallying the troops, seducing a significant other, comforting a parent, or pleading for the life of a son. Different goals require different alignments. You do not sit in a pub the same way as at the family table on Thanksgiving. In each setting, your goals are very different. So, the actor needs a general alignment that makes possible the widest number of specific alignments to fit particular situations. In other words, a proper general alignment is one that allows the body to organize and reorganize freely and readily according to the different situational goals required of the actor from one part of the script or scenario to the next.

Alignment is closely associated with grounding and balance. In fact, alignment may even be placed ahead of grounding. (When you work through this chapter a second time, you might want to start with alignment and move backward.) But placing alignment at the end of this first work-through was not an arbitrary choice. Alignment determines indirectly how our bodies look to others from one moment to the next. Therefore, deal-

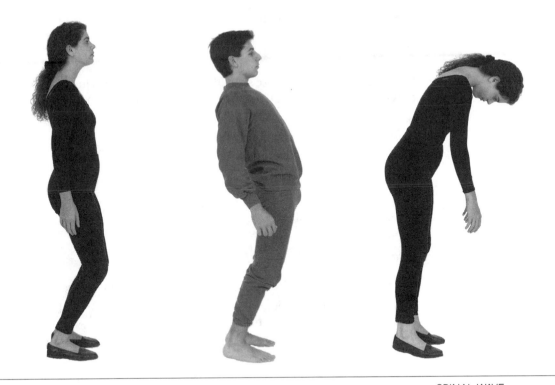

SPINAL WAVE.

ing with alignment first could easily encourage some to focus directly on how they look rather than on how their bodies are working.

A good actor's alignment is seldom a cosmetic issue. Rather, it is an issue of personal power. The sense of power a character conveys is related directly to the actor's ability to organize his or her physical resources in accord with the character's specific goals. For example, an actor playing a spy who is eavesdropping on a conversation must manage his or her body in such a way as to overhear every word without being detected. An alignment that creates only an attractive posture is useless. Actually, there is an important paradox in all of this. Balanced, well-grounded alignments often end up making you look more alive, responsive, and appealing than purely cosmetic postures that turn you into a life-size glossy of a real human being.[3]

Exercise 1–27: Spinal Wave

1. Pretend you are standing close to a wall made of paper.
2. Touch the imaginary wall first with your knees, then with your belt buckle, next with your chest, then with your chin, and finally with the top of your forehead.

3. When done in succession, these movements should produce a single undulation that begins with bending the knees and ends with the head flopping loosely forward.

Guidelines: This exercise should be done *gently,* with just enough vigor to require a short step or two at the end to keep you from tipping forward.

Exercise 1–28: Grounding the Wave

1. After you have become familiar with the wave, do it with particular attention to relaxing as much as possible, especially in the neck and shoulders.
2. After each wave, be sure to loosen the muscles in your feet and lower legs and make full contact with the floor.

Exercise 1–29: The Vocal Wave

1. Choose any of the following vowel sounds: ah, oh, ee, oo.
2. As the wave rises through your body, let the sound rise in pitch and volume. This should be done in one sustained breath.
3. It is important to avoid strain. Pitch and volume will rise with just a little encouragement on your part.
4. Pay attention to the sensations your voice creates in your body and to how it changes the way you do the wave.

Exercise 1–30: Loosening Up

1. Sit with your legs crossed and your upper torso straight but loose.
2. Attend to your breathing for a few moments, recalling the image of your torso as a cylinder.
3. As you exhale, think of loosening your body and extending the crown of your head (between the ears) gently upward. (Avoid hyperextension by retaining the feeling of relaxation and looseness in your back and neck as you extend.)
4. Because loosening and exhaling are often associated with collapsing, you may find the upward movement a little awkward. But relaxation need not require the loss of personal form and structural integrity.

Exercise 1–31: The Arch

1. Sit with your legs folded and your chin on your chest so your shoulders and back are rounded.
2. As you exhale, move the small of your back forward gently, so that your spine straightens comfortably.

THE ARCH, STEP 3.
The movements for this
exercise are small and
gentle. Feel your
shoulders loosen and
move back.

3. Guide the process by lifting your head simultaneously and pointing your nose toward the ceiling at roughly a 45° angle.
4. As your torso rises, allow your shoulders to shift back and your back to arch *slightly*.
5. Repeat the exercise four or five times.

Exercise 1–32: The Lift

1. Lie on your back with your knees up, soles on the floor, feet 12"–18" apart.
2. Notice what parts of your back and pelvis make contact with the floor.
3. Relax by letting go of tight back muscles when you exhale.
4. Imagine you have a tail coming out the bottom of your spine.
5. Pretend that someone picks up your tail and lifts your spine slowly off the ground so that your back rises one vertebra at a time up to the part directly between your shoulder blades.
6. Your imaginary companion then restores your back to its original position, again one vertebra at a time.
7. Try to feel where one vertebra ends and the next begins.
8. Do this exercise three or four times; then lie still and review the way your back makes contact with the floor.

Guidelines: Do this exercise gently, without forcing the arch in your back to become too big.

Exercise 1–33: Arm Pull I

1. Kneel on your right knee and extend your right arm straight up.

THE LIFT, STEP 5.

2. Take your right wrist with your left hand.

3. Use your left arm to pull yourself gently to your feet.

4. Exhale as you rise, looking up at the wrist as you pull.

Exercise 1–34: Arm Pull II

1. Kneel on your left knee and extend your left arm.

2. Take your left wrist in your right hand.

3. Continue as above.

Exercise 1–35: Implicating the Voice

1. Repeat the last two exercises, remembering to rise up as you exhale.

2. Try to discover a sound that makes pulling yourself to your feet feel easier or more comfortable.

3. Imagine that the pulling upward is actually causing your voice to sound.

Guidelines: Because it is part of the body, the voice will change as your alignment changes. Therefore, it is important not to strain. The pulling and standing should be fluid and easy.

NOTES

1. This and the next two exercises are standard bioenergetic protocols. I have adapted them from the work of Alexander Lowen and Patricia Relf.

2. I owe this and the next exercise to Zbignew Cynkutis of the Polish Laboratorium.

3. Besides the sources I have already mentioned (Cynkutis, Feldenkrais, Lowen, Alexander), I owe the inspiration for and some of the moves in the following exercises to William Kuhlke, my colleague at the University of Kansas.

REFERENCES

Feldenkrais, Moshe. *Awareness Through Movement: Health Exercises for Personal Growth.* New York: Harper and Row, 1977. The emphasis is on practical exercises that apply Feldenkrais's ideas about the relationship between healthy human functioning and physical structure. For a more extensive explanation of the theory behind his exercises, read the next two books.

———. *Body and Mature Behavior: A Study of Anxiety, Sex, Gravitation, and Learning.* Madison, CT: International Universities Press, 1949. The author includes a brief chapter on the relationship between the body and emotion.

———. *The Potent Self: A Guide to Spontaneity.* Edited by Michaeleen Kimmey. New York: Harper and Row, 1985. Feldenkrais links personal potential to a well-integrated physical and emotional life.

Grotowski, Jerzy. *Towards a Poor Theatre.* New York: Simon and Schuster, 1968. This volume is really a collection of notes and interviews with and by a variety of people. Although unsystematic, the anthology describes many of the assumptions and protocols used by the Polish Laboratorium in the late fifties and sixties.

Lowen, Alexander. *Bioenergetics.* New York: Penguin Books, 1975. An introduction to bioenergetics for lay people, this book explains the principles of bioenergetics using several examples and exercises.

———. *The Language of the Body.* New York: Collier Macmillan Books, 1958. Using some of the language of classical psychoanalysis, Lowen presents a detailed discussion and defense of the major assumptions underlying bioenergetics. The book is directed at Lowen's fellow psychiatrists and psychologists.

Relf, Patricia. "The Application of Bioenergetic Theory and Technique to Actor Training." Ph.D. dissertation, Bowling Green State University, 1976. This study does exactly what its title says.

*(Notes, ideas,
sketches, reactions
to the exercises . . .)*

_____

_____

_____

_____

_____

_____

_____

_____

_____

_____

_____

_____

_____

_____

_____

_____

_____

_____

_____

_____

*(Notes, ideas,
sketches, reactions
to the exercises . . .)*

*(Notes, ideas,
sketches, reactions
to the exercises . . .)*

_____

_____

_____

_____

_____

_____

_____

_____

_____

_____

_____

_____

_____

_____

_____

_____

_____

_____

_____

Openness

Openness is the capacity to be vulnerable—that is, to allow events in our surroundings to have an impact on us. The world on stage supplies a steady shower of stimuli that, if we let them, can provoke lively and useful responses. To truly hear and let in the insults of another actor/character is to ignite the burners of our anger, which, in turn, helps us inflame others. On stage, an actor must take in, in order to give back. But the old wisdom that acting is really reacting becomes a frigid cliché without some assessment of what is required to allow honest, organic reactions to take form and drive us toward doing. Openness is not automatic, based only on deciding, "Now I'll be open for two hours." Openness—the ability to take in and use the energy in our environment—is an acquired skill.

At a fairly young age most of us discovered that the world sometimes produces painful sensations and arouses disturbing feelings. You and I learned to protect ourselves to some extent by closing off. This closing was, and continues to be, more than metaphorical. It was and is organic. In the face of painful experience, we constrict our muscles and shift our postures to form a protective shield and/or lock in the emotional responses we know no one wants to deal with. Our present muscular habits are both part of our attempt to shield ourselves and part of the way we keep "the lid on" our feelings. Our big brothers may have all grown into nice guys, but the muscular organization of our legs may be the product of a childhood need to flee from their wrath at a moment's notice. And our stomach and neck muscles may retain the residue of the tension that helped us suppress the giggles an exasperated teacher did not want to hear.

[T]he moment anything is a success it must be abandoned. If not, it becomes set and closed. . . .
JOHN HEILPERN,
CONFERENCE OF THE BIRDS

Everything, stage, setting, costume, speaking, creative acting [must be] in a state of finding; of not expecting fresh solutions, but keeping open.
J. C. TREWIN,
PETER BROOK: A BIOGRAPHY

As Stanley Keleman notes in his book, *Emotional Anatomy,* we wear our past lives in the form of certain anatomical organizations that we took on as an adaptation to unfavorable events. *These organizations are the physical imprint of experience and form the basis for our emotional lives.* The physical and the emotional accompany one another and are part of one another. We blush with (not from) embarrassment, freeze with terror, and become sick with revulsion. Moreover, since we live in our bodies every day and are accustomed to them, we are generally unaware of the overactive and/or underactive muscular dynamics that reduce the vividness of our experience and the range of our feelings.

Not every experience leads to a pattern of muscular armor that becomes a habit over time. Many of life's experiences are positive and can have a benign effect on our bodies, helping the muscles to retain their suppleness and sensitivity to neural impulses. But as normal people living in the real world, our personal histories are seldom filled only with "poly-unsaturated" glee. We have all been altered in some way by disagreeable experiences.

EXERCISES

The following exercises stretch and loosen habitually constricted muscle groups and activate those that are chronically flaccid. By freeing muscular formations that have been organized over time to inhibit our awareness and expression of feeling, the exercises help us develop a more vivid emotional life. The associations and memories that accompany our emotional lives also become richer and more distinct.

A little work each day is better than great gobs once in a while. These exercises require a sense of respect for yourself. Be gentle and do the work simply and honestly.

The Eight Circles

The first sequence of exercises is based on Grotowski's *exercises plastiques.* Like so many theatre exercises, these address a number of issues, including balance, alignment, and security. But, whatever else they may do, they also contribute powerfully to openness. The *plastiques* re-form muscle groups away from the unnecessary and chronic patterns of contraction and decontraction that inhibit physical and emotional response. Muscles no longer obligated to protect and suppress are free to become motile and react to whatever the world offers.

Before beginning, remind yourself that the circles do not carry any emotional obligation. You don't have to make yourself feel any particular way. Just do the exercise with whatever feelings happen to occur.

Exercise 2–1: Head Circles

1. Take an open, fully grounded stance.
2. *Gently* revolve your head while loosening your neck muscles.
3. Imagine your neck muscles are stretching so that your head makes larger circles.
4. After three or four circles, stop. Wait a moment and do the same number of circles in the opposite direction. Stop and rest again.

Exercise 2–2: Including Other Muscle Groups

1. Repeat the exercise.
2. This time make six to ten gentle circles, first clockwise then counter-clockwise.
3. Allow the movement of your head to seep into the rest of your body gently and gradually. Allow the movement of the rest of your body to work in a way that makes the head circles free, playful, and pleasant.
4. Stop *before* you become dizzy. You can always go back to the exercise after a brief rest.

Exercise 2–3: Head and Voice

1. Begin the circles again, allowing the rest of your body to help.
2. Allow the movement to evoke a sound from your voice.
3. Try to find a sound that makes the movement feel freer and looser. The sound of the voice is an altogether natural product of the body's motion. Sometimes it takes more effort and tension to keep silent than it does to put voice into your movement. So, try to produce the sound by simply "letting go" of your voice.
4. Concentrate on how your body *feels* as it moves and creates sound rather than on how you want others to see and hear you.

Exercise 2–4: Shoulder Circles

1. Hold your left arm away from your side a little.
2. Imagine a small hoop placed vertically around your left shoulder so it passes between your arm and torso.

SHOULDER CIRCLES.
The image of the hoop
will help keep your move-
ment circular.

3. Rotate your shoulder so it traces a large circle along the inside edge of the hoop.

4. Repeat the exercise with your right shoulder.

Exercise 2–5: Sound and Motion: Shoulders

1. Now, make twenty to thirty forward rotations with both shoulders together.

2. Allow the movement to seep into the rest of your body and evoke sound. Remember, the movement of the rest of your body and your voice should help make the rotations easier and more pleasant.

3. Make ten to fifteen backward circles.

4. Next, do ten circles in each direction, one shoulder at a time.

5. Finally, make ten to fifteen circles with both shoulders moving in opposite directions at the same time. (Good luck!)

6. Throughout the exercise let the speed and size of the circles vary with the movement of the rest of the body and the sound. In other words, let the exercise vary naturally and work for free, playful movement.

Exercise 2–6: Hip Circles

1. Put the hoop around your hips horizontally.
2. Using the hoop as your guide, make three or four circles in each direction.
3. Work for precision.

Exercise 2–7: Sound and Motion: Hips

1. Make twenty to thirty hip circles in each direction.
2. Allow the movement to seep into your body and allow your voice to join in.
3. Once again, allow the size, rate, and intensity of all the movements to vary.

Exercise 2–8: Torso Circles

1. Move the hoop up to your chest.
2. Put your hands on your hips and make a large horizontal circle with your chest, first in one direction, then in the other.

TORSO CIRCLES.
Placing your hands on
your hips helps to keep
them centered, which
allows for better balance
throughout the exercise.

Exercise 2–9: Sound and Motion: Torso

1. Make twenty to thirty torso circles in each direction.
2. Allow the rest of your body and your voice to join in, helping to make the movement free, pleasant, and playful.
3. Vary the qualities of the sound and movement as you work.

Exercise 2–10: Knee Circles

1. Follow the same pattern but with the hoop around your knees. Have your feet together.

Exercise 2–11: Sound and Motion: Knees

1. Use the same procedure as in the last two sound and motion exercises.
2. Vary the exercise by changing the width of your stance.

Exercise 2–12: Foot and Leg Rotation

1. Raise one foot 6″–10″ off the ground.

FOOT AND LEG
ROTATION.
Think of your ankle as
a pivot.

2. Rotate your foot from the ankle, tracing a circle with your big toe.

3. Do twenty to thirty circles one way, then the other. Include your voice.

4. Now, make twenty to thirty more circles, moving the entire lower leg from the knee. Make sure you are still tracing the circle with your big toe.

5. Change legs and repeat the exercise.

Exercise 2–13: Arm Circles

1. Extend your left arm horizontally. Put the hoop around your left elbow.

2. Rotate your arm so as to trace a circle along the inside edge of the hoop.

3. Make several circles with that arm, then switch to the other. Next, make circles with both arms simultaneously.

4. Let your entire body including your voice help you make the circles. Be sure to change the speed, size, and direction of the circles.

Exercise 2–14: Hand Circles

1. Raise your right arm above your head. Open your hand but keep the fingers and thumb together.

2. Rotate your hand from the wrist, making several circles. Switch arms and make several circles with that hand. Then make circles with both hands together.

HAND CIRCLES.
Keep the motion light
and vary the speed.

3. As usual, allow your voice and the rest of your body to support the movement of your hands.

If done precisely and with enough variation in speed, size, and intensity, these exercises can begin to reorganize major muscle groups and deepen your emotional life. The trick is to maintain the shape of the circles. What you are thinking about as you do the circles is very important because your mental activity can change the way the exercises work on you. For the first few times, you might have to focus on the form of the exercise—that is, follow the instructions accurately. But there is no reason to get stuck on this plateau. Soon the exercises become easy.

Concentrate on how your body feels as you move and sound. When you are able to concentrate on your body states, take a moment at the end of each exercise to stand still and develop a loose and settled feeling in the muscle group you have been working with.

It is also important to experiment frequently with a third kind of concentration. *As you do each of the circles,* instead of attending to the muscles that are doing most of the work, try to discover muscle groups that could be more relaxed than they are. Release those areas that seem to be holding *unnecessary* tension. (Keep in mind, however, that not all tension is unnecessary—a perfectly relaxed person would fall down. Unnecessary tension is the kind that overtaxes the body and reduces its adaptability.) The discoveries can be interesting. For example, I often find that I tighten the muscles in one of my forearms and hands when I'm working with my torso. When I loosen the extra tension, it almost always springs up somewhere else—in my other hand or in one of my feet. My body is so addicted to certain sorts of tension that I cannot let it go without it cropping up in another area. The tension once meant emotional protection and self-control. So letting go of my holding patterns has meant risking a change in how I experience myself in the world. But freedom can be scary. Unconscious fears and constraints will not go away with a few swings of the hips; the process is long term.

A fourth level of concentration is on the inner life (feelings, associations, memories) that the exercises evoke. There is no need to hurry. This fourth level will come naturally if you maintain the *plastiques* as part of your daily regimen.

To be an actor requires great faith and courage. You must be willing to challenge the limits the world has imprinted upon your body and emotional structure. Acting also requires a keen sense of self-respect. The limited motility or constriction you carry in some muscle groups is there because at one time you needed it. You cannot force openness. Try not to become addicted to pain. Take your time. Great acting is open and free; also, it is full of great joy.

Dynamic Flow

In general, dynamic flow is simply moving from one of the eight circles to another without pausing. The goal is to allow new relationships to develop among the muscle groups by finding a variety of non-habitual "pathways" from one circle to the next. There is no need to figure out beforehand how to get from one to another. Just do each exercise and trust your body to make the discoveries. Dynamic flow can contribute a great deal to the variety of your movement as well as to your emotional range. In my own work, I notice that dynamic flow stimulates my inner life to change more frequently and to be generally more upbeat.

Exercise 2–15: Sequence I

1. Start with head circles. Make sure to use a stance that creates a sense of stability.

2. Allow the head circles to become shoulder circles,

3. which become torso circles;

4. which become hip circles;

5. then knee circles;

6. next foot circles,

7. then arm circles,

8. and finally hand circles.

Guidelines: Remember not to stop between each step. Dynamic flow is really just an expansion on something you have already done in the previous exercises: allowing the movement of one muscle group to "seep" into other parts of the body. Repeat sequence I frequently, until you can go from step 1 to step 8 easily. There is no need to hurry.

Exercise 2–16: Sequence II

1. Repeat the preceding exercise, incorporating your voice and allowing your motion to move you around a little.

DYNAMIC FLOW, *continued.*

2. Try to find out which transitions feel awkward or uncomfortable. Work with these transitions by changing your voice when you get to them. Think of movement from one circle to the next as letting go (or releasing) into the new motion.

Exercise 2–17: Sequence III

1. Change the order of the circles, beginning with step 8 and going to step 1. Make sure to keep your voice and movement free and relaxed.

2. Increase the variation in the size and speed of the circles. Use more of the room when your momentum requires it.

3. Vary the rhythm and intensity of the work. You can be relaxed and energetic at the same time. In a well-organized body, the two reinforce one another.

Guidelines: Now, here's the trap. When you are working with others, you may begin to focus on how you look or sound, and a competitiveness can set in. It is no crime to have an ego—but don't let it defeat you. Discipline your concentration so that you can focus on the sensations you are experiencing instead of on what you want others to see and hear. Linger over the first three sequences until you can keep your concentration on what the movement is doing to you. Once you can tune into the sensations you are creating in your body, you are ready to vary the style of your concentration.

The following exercises explore the impact of three other kinds of concentration: on associations, on memories, and on feelings.

Exercise 2–18: Flow Guided by Associations

1. Begin by doing the flow sequence. Start with any circle you wish and move freely from one to the next. Include your voice.

2. As you work be alert for whatever images come up—for example, a room full of Pepsi Cola bubbles changing to a sea of pink champagne which becomes a huge scarlet pillow. Have a good time.

3. Continue your work under the influence of your images.

4. Each image should serve as background music, triggering variations in the rhythm, speed, size, and intensity of your sound and motion.

Exercise 2–19: Flow Guided by Memories

1. Do the exercise again, allowing whatever memories occur to become vivid.

Exercise 2–20: Flow Guided by Feelings

1. Repeat the same exercise again.

2. This time become aware of whatever emotions crop up during your work.

If you've been working through this book systematically, these last three exercises probably seem fairly straightforward—the natural next step. But they are nonetheless crucial because they underscore the need to create a connection between the inner and outer life of the actor. At one time, it was popular to think of each in terms of cause and effect. If the body were trained, the mind would cause it to express inner life. The mind acted upon the body, not vice versa. Now things have changed. It is becoming more common to view mind and body as related functions rather than separate faculties—related functions that work together and influence one another. Mind and body are two sides of the same coin. But what do we call the coin: the self? the human system? What word expresses the singleness of body and mind? A colleague has pointed out that in Japanese the character

mind

body

unity

means mind-body and gets at the notion of duality-in-one. But our own language is not so lucky. A hyphen between words will have to do.

Opening the Voice

Like the rest of your body, your voice is only half your own. It is shaped and constrained by the circumstances in which you first made sounds. In

EXPANDING THE
ACTION OF THE
TORSO, STEP 4.
Be gentle with your head
and neck and concen-
trate primarily on the
sensations in your torso
when you breathe.

part, the voice you have now is the audible evidence of how others responded to your early utterances. In a loud environment, your softer sounds may have been discouraged. Your vocal habits may still reflect the effort it took to make yourself heard when you were younger. The way your voice works, then, is partially a product of the social environment that imprinted your body with its lasting effects.

An important dimension of the actor's work, therefore, is to undo the vocal habits that reduce the power, versatility, and communicativeness of the voice. A person who is in full possession of his or her body-voice system is very powerful. Such an individual can communicate in a way that makes the rest of us hear, feel, think, and sense much that we might want to avoid. While performing, a trained actor uses an expressive capacity freed from the usual, unconscious constraints that plague the rest of us.

The relationship between audience and actor is paradoxical. In order to represent the human community, the actor attempts to free himself or herself from the very inhibitions the community imposes as the price of membership—a price that makes its members predictable and less powerful in the course of their daily lives. Great actors are examples to us all of what we can do.

Exercise 2–21: Expanding the Action of the Torso

1. Take a moment to loosen and relax.

2. Lie on your left side, using your left arm as a cushion for your head.

3. Now reach up with your right hand and cup your left ear.

4. Lift your head with your hand four or five times. As you lift, notice the sensations in your back and sides created by your breathing.

Exercise 2–22: Varying the Work of the Torso

1. Keeping your head down on your arm, lift your right leg four or five times, once again noticing the sensations on both sides and on your back.

Exercise 2–23: Integrating Muscular Action

1. Now combine both exercises. Lift your head (using your right hand) and your right leg simultaneously.

2. Incorporate your voice by making a sound that makes the movement easier.

Exercise 2–24: Circling Back

1. Turn on your right side and repeat the last three exercises.

Exercise 2–25: "Ah"

1. Lie on your back with your knees up and your feet on the floor.

2. Relax tight muscles by exhaling and letting go.

3. Make five or six "ah" sounds. Try to develop a sense of ease and looseness in your throat and neck.

Exercise 2–26: Reclaiming Your Voice

1. Remain on your back with your knees up.

2. As you exhale, instead of "ah," say quietly to yourself: "This is my voice."

3. Make the statement several times, speaking softly to yourself.

4. Focus on whatever associations and feelings come up—however fleeting they may be.

Exercise 2–27: Deepening Your Voice Work

1. Now change the script to "I have a right to my own voice." Continue to speak softly, to yourself.

Exercise 2–28: Sharing Awareness with Others

1. Sit opposite a partner or in a circle with other actors.
2. Turn "This is my voice" into a dialogue with a second actor by repeating the line to one another.
3. Alter the pitch, volume, speed, and tone with which you say the line to one another. In other words, experiment freely.
4. But after each experiment, come back to your own natural vocal dynamics.
5. The emphasis should be on *reaching out* to the other actor by means of your voice.

Exercise 2–29: Varying the Contact

1. Move around the room.
2. Do short dialogues ("This is my voice") with other members of the class whom you encounter as you move.
3. After a few minutes, change your script to one of the following:
   "Listen to my voice."
   "This is my voice and it's soft enough."
   "This is my voice and it's loud enough."
4. Try changing from one line to another, but use no more than one line for each encounter. After each actor has uttered one line, move on to someone else.

Guidelines: As you work through the last two exercises, you may find that your habitual tension and inhibition come flooding back, or you may discover an impulse to race and pump up your energy level. In either case, stop and go back to the full, gentle 360° breathing you have been working on. Then resume the exercise. You are under no obligation to have specific feelings, images, or associations, or to get a particular response from anyone. Just do the exercise with integrity, making an effort to contact others with your voice.

Exercise 2–30: Throat and Neck Release

1. Sit with the soles of your feet together. Tilt your head back a little.

2. Grip your throat gently so that your thumb and forefinger are about one inch below the jawline.

3. Massage the sides of your neck by pressing in *gently* and moving your fingers in small, slow circles. Continue this massage for about one minute. At the same time, slowly nod your head forward and back.

Exercise 2–31: The Sigh

1. Continue the exercise.

2. Inhale gently and sigh a full "ah" without trying to control the pitch or quality of the sound. Let it be influenced by the massage and movement of your head.

Exercise 2–32: The Cry

1. Now, sigh an "ah" four or five times.

2. Let each sound grow in fullness and amplitude.

3. Don't strain for volume. Instead, work at relaxing your neck and breathing deeply. Your aim should be to free the sound rather than to force it out.

Exercise 2–33: Voice and Upper Body Release

1. Have your partner stand behind you and press down with his or her hands on the top of your shoulders.

This is your starting position just before your partner enters the picture.

2. When you feel the pressure beginning to bend your knees, break away from your partner.

3. As you break away, say *one* of the following core statements:

"Get off my back."

"Let me go."

"I'm sick of carrying you."

4. The movement to free yourself and the statement should be eruptive and simultaneous.

Exercise 2–34: Voice and Stomach Release

1. Lie on your back with your legs straight and your ankles more or less together. Your partner should stand next to your knees facing you.

2. Place your arms at your sides a short distance from your body with your palms down on the floor.

3. Lift your head and shoulders off the floor and breathe as normally as possible.

4. Hold this position while your partner extends his or her hand toward your face *as though* to cover your mouth and press your head down. (*Under no circumstances should this action actually be completed.*) It's the suggestion that counts.

5. Strike your partner's hand away from your face, and allow the motion to roll you onto your stomach. As you swing, make one of these core statements:

"Get out of my face."

"Get out of my sight."

"No!"

Guidelines: Again the movement and statement should be eruptive.

Exercise 2–35: Releasing Pelvis and Voice

1. Lie on your back with your knees up and the soles of your feet on the floor about 12″–15″ apart.

2. Lift your legs up and turn your feet into a slightly pigeon-toed position. Bend your knees against your chest.

3. Your partner should move toward your feet as though to push you over backward. Again, no contact should be made.

4. Kick out hard toward your partner and say:

   "Get away from me."

   "Leave me alone."[1]

Our voices are intimately associated with our chest, stomach, and pelvic muscles. These same three muscle groups are largely responsible for guaranteeing our physical safety. Working with the voice in relationship to these muscle groups and our need for safety contributes to vocal freedom.

NOTES

1. I learned the last three exercises from Kevin Kuhlke, who teaches acting at N.Y.U.

REFERENCES

Heilpern, John. *Conference of the Birds*. New York: Penguin, 1977.

Keleman, Stanley. *Embodying Experience: Forming a Personal Life*. Berkeley, California: Center Press, 1987. "This book is about the life of the body, the role of the emotions, and man's search for meaning. It suggests how to disassemble outmoded behavior, assemble the elements of experience into new behavior, and how to use yourself to influence personal destiny" (p. 2). While written largely from a clinical point of view, the book's theme of human potential extends its applicability beyond those who suffer from serious psychological problems.

————. *Emotional Anatomy*. Berkeley, CA: Center Press, 1985. The writing is fairly technical, but the book stakes out a somewhat untraditional way of looking at the human body. Keleman emphasizes the liquid and kinetic (moving) elements of anatomy. The book tries to show how the shape a person has—that is, how he or she is organized—helps to determine both psychological and social functioning.

————. *Patterns of Distress: Emotional Insults and Human Form*. Berkeley, CA: Center Press, 1989. Keleman describes the various ways a person responds to challenges and insults from the social environment. The emphasis is on the physical and emotional dynamics of those responses.

Rolfe, Ida Pauline. *Rolfing, the Interpretation of Human Structures*. Santa Monica, CA: Dennis-Landman, 1977.

Trewin, J. C. *Peter Brook: A Biography*. London: Macdonald, 1971.

*(Notes, ideas,
sketches, reactions
to the exercises . . .)*

*(Notes, ideas,
sketches, reactions
to the exercises . . .)*

_____

_____

_____

_____

_____

_____

_____

_____

_____

_____

_____

_____

_____

_____

_____

_____

_____

_____

_____

_____

_____

_____

(Notes, ideas, sketches, reactions to the exercises . . .)

Stillness

Stillness holds interest for anyone willing to listen. When I remain awake and still for a period of time the imaginative journeys extend far. . . . There is a definite correlation between the time spent in stillness and the amount of imaginative activity resulting.

MARY O'DONNELL
FULKERSON,
THE MOVE TO STILLNESS

In part, *stillness is a combination of relaxation and readiness.* I know this may seem paradoxical since in our everyday usage relaxation and readiness are not generally connected. But stillness is not a typical condition. It has to be cultivated. The relaxation that is part of stillness is not the flaccid, semicomatose state associated with summer, hammocks, beer, and barbecue. In the context of performance, relaxation is the absence of unnecessary muscular tension—the state in which we are most in control of those resources that support energetic behavior. Readiness is simply part of this kind of relaxation. It is the willingness to rise to any occasion, a predisposition to react confidently to any stimulus. Balance, alignment, a sense of ground, muscular motility—all the material in the first two chapters—contribute to stillness since they help to develop the right kind of relaxation and the readiness to do.

Besides relaxation and readiness, stillness also includes a particular way of concentrating on our experience in the moment. Stillness includes the capacity to devote our attention fully to what is happening in the *now* of our lives. In any one instant, we can focus on whatever is going on, or we can escape into a host of concerns that insulate us from living our experiences fully. On stage there are many distractions from what is happening in the moment. We can worry about how we look or sound to the audience, whether we are being funny enough or sad enough. We can work on pumping up our feelings, obsess over our next lines or a piece of business. All of these defensive preoccupations constitute a kind of ongoing "noise" that inhibits our attention to the life around us and what it evokes in us.

Stillness quiets the internal noise and helps us to tune in to what is happening. It is really a mode of respect for what experience offers—a respect that defers our addiction to our own internal "musak" in favor of attending to what is knocking on the door of our consciousness trying to become part of our immediate life. For actors, letting awareness take hold and stimulate a response is an essential skill.

You cannot worry about quieting your internal noise while in the midst of a performance. Thus, the purpose of the following exercises is to help you make stillness a habit that replaces other habits, specifically those that take you out of the moment or short-circuit your responses to what is going on.

EXERCISES

Quieting the Noise

Inside all of us is quite a hubbub—a bedlam of activity that comes between us and the stimuli that surround us. Here is a way to quiet things down a little in order to concentrate more completely.

Exercise 3–1: Attention (visual focus)

1. Set up a breathing rate slower than your normal one. Try inhaling to a four count and exhaling to a five count. Prolonging the exhalation by one count will help keep you from hyperventilating.
2. Now look at some simple object—a tree outside your window, the wall in front of you, just about anything will do.
3. Try to stay focused on the object. If thoughts or associations occur, neither resist nor indulge them. Just allow yourself to notice them; then go back to your original object. (Struggling against mental or emotional activity is just another way to create noise.)
4. As you dwell on the object, try to notice as many details about it as possible.
5. Repeat this exercise two or three times (with breaks between each session). Each time try to increase the number of details you observe.

Exercise 3–2: Attention (auditory focus)

1. Choose a sound in your environment, something simple—the buzz of an appliance, children playing in the distance, whatever sound is fairly constant.
2. Set up a breathing rate as in the previous exercise and focus on the sound. If images, sensations, associations, and so on crop up, notice them; then return your attention to the sound.

I found that the chief difficulty for most people was to realize that they had really heard "new things": that is, things that they had never heard before. They kept translating what they heard into their habitual language.

OUSPENSKY, QUOTED BY BABA RAM DASS IN *REMEMBER, BE HERE NOW*

3. Repeat the exercise, attempting to increase the number of changes you can detect in what you hear.

Exercise 3–3: Attention (kinesthetic focus)

1. Try to discover your dominant physical sensation. It may be the pressure of your buttocks on the floor or chair, the feeling of your elbows on the table, the touch of your clothing against your skin.
2. Follow the same steps as for the last two exercises.

Many of us are addicted to our own noise, so these exercises may not come easily. However, there is nothing to be gained by becoming upset with lapses in your concentration, episodes of boredom, or frustration. It is normal to encounter a little resistance to change. Try to deal with it peacefully. Set yourself a time limit, say five to seven minutes. If you can't get back on track within your time limit, stop and try again later.

Awareness and Self-Image

Everything that happens to us on a particular day becomes a part of us. Unfortunately, we often evaluate ourselves and our day in terms of the one or two experiences that seem to stand out. As a result, we all too easily end up characterizing ourselves in a one-dimensional way: "winners," "losers," "successes at the game of life," "victims of the game," and so on. Using one or two occurrences to characterize a whole day's worth of experiences creates a simplistic sense of self that makes it hard to develop a broad and varied emotional life.

To help ward off a limited perspective on ourselves and form the basis for a more complex, multidimensional self-image, we can develop a daily inventory of as many experiences as we can recall. Such an inventory helps build up a storehouse of memories, each with its own emotional valence—memories that can be evoked by something in a script, or by another actor, or by a director.

Exercise 3–4: Detail Recollection

1. Walk around the room a bit more slowly than normal.
2. While you walk try to recall as much of your day as possible, starting when you awoke and moving to the present moment.
3. Remember as many details as you can and notice what feelings and associations occur with the memories.

Exercise 3–5: Meeting Yourself in the Moment

1. Make an appointment with yourself.

2. When the assigned time comes, find a private place and answer the following questions:

   What am I doing right now?

   What am I feeling?

   What do I want?

   What do I expect?

   What would I like to avoid?

3. Now, make an appointment with a character you would like to play. Pose the same questions.

The purpose of the next exercise is, first, to help you focus on your own experience as it changes and unfolds and, second, to give you the chance to enjoy being honest about what is happening to you without having to explain yourself to others.

Exercise 3–6: Moment-to-Moment Awareness

1. Sit on the floor with your legs crossed or with the soles of your feet together.

2. Breathe slowly but comfortably.

3. Now, express your moment-to-moment awarenesses out loud. For the first few statements, use the form, "I am aware of (or that) . . . " Keep the statements as simple as possible.

4. Some of your awarenesses may be of external reality, such as the color of a wall or the sound of someone else's breathing. Other awarenesses may be internal, such as feelings of confusion, delight, worry, satisfaction, and so on, or associations in the form of images or impulses.

Guidelines: You can do this exercise individually or in a group, in a normal voice or very quietly.

Here is an example of the exercise, written on June 21, 1985, at 9:55 in the morning:

1. I am aware of taking a deep breath as I begin this exercise.

2. I am aware of the tension I feel between wishing to be honest and wanting my privacy.

3. I am aware of feeling cautious and hesitant about what I'm writing.

4. I'm stuck.

5. Now, I notice the large, very green sycamore tree outside my living-room window.

6. I hear my children arguing about how to spend their day.

7. I feel some anger about the interruption.

8. I am aware of wanting to "perform" this exercise. I want to make it and me sound profound and exciting.

It is important to avoid rationalizations or explanations. Focus on sensations, feelings, and associations. Do not worry about where they come from, why they are occurring, or what value judgments you might make of them. These issues are irrelevant, at least for this exercise. When you can no longer continue, you have reached impasse—an inability to concentrate, a feeling of being stuck, bored, or just plain frustrated. Impasse means you are on the verge of breaking through to some new awarenesses that are perhaps too deeply personal or too amorphous for you to form into words. Stop when you can go no further. Impasse will not go away just because you want it to. The best strategy is simply to come back to the exercise frequently. Eventually, the new awarenesses will take form, and you will be able to continue your list.

For the actor on stage, being engaged in the here and now is a precious state, for it is the source of the energy and danger that all great acting must possess. To commit to the moment is to run the risk of forgetting lines, staging, the director's plan—all the structural components of production that make us feel secure. But the structure of a production arrived at through trial, error, memorization, and systematic decisions is like an intricately woven trampoline. The tighter the weave, the greater the potential for flight. There can be no flying, however, until you let go of the trampoline and commit yourself to living moment to moment in thin air. Stillness is the first step.

Exercise 3–7: Bipolar Awareness

1. Sit across from a partner.

2. Concentrate on one another for a few moments.

3. Then do the previous exercise as a dialogue. For example:

> A: "I'm aware of how nervous I am about doing this exercise with you."
>
> B: "I noticed you looked away while you were talking."
>
> A: "I'm aware of how much I don't want to do this now."
>
> B: "I feel a little guilty—like it's my fault you're having trouble."

Guidelines: Once again, when impasse occurs, respect it and stop. It is useless to continue by inventing statements that really have nothing to do with what you're experiencing.

The image produced by this exercise—two actors engaged in an ongoing process of honest communication—is important. Of course, in a traditional production, you will be saying someone else's words, and you may be using your body in an untypical way. But the words and movement must be more than cosmetic or arbitrary. They are your means of communicating with the other actor. No matter how stylized or nonrealistic a production may be, at a very basic level, the actors are engaged in something far more than a pretense. There must be real human exchange—the give and take of energy, what Stanislavski called "communion."

Free and honest give and take is the "raw material" of great acting—like the wonderful Carrara marble in the *Pietà*. To be sure the material must be shaped before it is ready for an audience. Without the basic human exchange between the actors, there is nothing to shape; or rather, there is shape without substance. Unless it is grounded on real communication and contact, acting becomes artificial, safe, devoid of warm-bodied humanity—a cynical parody of what is supposed to be most alive in live theatre. But more about contact in Chapter 5. For now, it is enough to focus on the stillness that will make contact possible.

REFERENCES

Alpert, Richard (Baba Ram Dass). *Remember, Be Here Now*. Albuquerque, NM: Modern Press, 1975 [first printing, 1971]. A book about many things, including a critique of certain life habits and ways of thinking we all pick up. It also contains yoga exercises and explanations of stillness from an Indian-Buddhist point of view.

Fulkerson, Mary O'Donnell. *The Move to Stillness*. Devon, England: Dartington College Theatre Department, 1982.

Jung, Carl G. *The Undiscovered Self*. Translated by R. F. C. Hull. New York: New American Library, 1957. Jung tries to pose a difference between a "real self" and a self distorted by modern technological culture. The attempt is worth reading because it points to ways socialization sometimes interferes with basic human processes. The book provides a realistic sense of how difficult stillness is to achieve.

Schutz, William C. *Joy: Expanding Human Awareness*. New York: Grove Press, 1967. Written to evoke a more intense awareness of immediate experience, Schutz's book supplies exercises and discussions that can expand the work begun in Part I.

*(Notes, ideas,
sketches, reactions
to the exercises . . .)*

_____

_____

_____

_____

_____

_____

_____

_____

_____

_____

_____

_____

_____

_____

_____

_____

_____

_____

_____

_____

(Notes, ideas, sketches, reactions to the exercises . . .)

*(Notes, ideas,
sketches, reactions
to the exercises . . .)*

*(Notes, ideas,
sketches, reactions
to the exercises . . .)*

The Given Circumstances

THE CIRCUS ON STAGE

In general, the "given circumstances" are the components of the play's fictive world—the who, what, where, when—that surround each character through every scene. They provoke and structure your responses in each moment of performance. The circus provides a useful analogy for how the given circumstances are supposed to work.

To accomplish their fabulous feats, trapeze flyers must depend completely on an ensemble of objects, people, and physical forces. Fly-bar and catch-bar must swing in sync. A catchman must spot and receive the flyer, and a guidesman tempers the tension and give in the wires and pulleys while the act is in progress so the rigging responds correctly to the flyer's velocity and weight. The astounding acrobatics are the outcome of a grand collusion between flyers and their given circumstances. Great aerialists know precisely how to use the support and energy of the special ecology that surrounds them.

A play provides different kinds of given circumstances, including other actors, particular arrangements of space and time, events, and a variety of costumes and objects. All of these contribute to the world of a play just as the pulleys, bars, catchmen, and so on contribute to the world of the trapeze act. In the theatre, as in the circus, the given circumstances are nonnegotiable gifts—nonnegotiable because they are generally thought of as integral parts of a play (you cannot just throw out the catchman and still do a triple or delete Claudius and still have Hamlet kill the king); and gifts because they operate as a readily available energy field that charges the work of those who know how to use them.

In life, as on stage, the world is given. But in life, unlike on stage, what is given is not always life-giving. In our daily routine, we must often duck some low-flying piece of the world determined to ruin our day. But in a performance, avoidance leads to self-destruction. The flyman who just hangs from the bar eventually falls, done in by gravity and the weight of his own independence. The actor who refuses to engage the given circumstances has nothing to react to and cuts himself off from all sources of supportive energy. We must meet the world on stage with a warm embrace, in order to gain what it has to give us. The same given circumstances that destroy Hamlet also help the actor playing him to perform a brilliant death scene.

DEFINING THE GIVEN CIRCUMSTANCES

The next few paragraphs are a basic description of the given circumstances. Frankly, this description is a device, a platform on which to stage the rest of Part II. Although subsequent chapters will flesh out the outline considerably, some of the most important additions will come from your work with the exercises. Every acting text is "rewritten" by the daily work of students and teachers.

Agents (Others). *Whoever is with you on stage. The other actor/character in a scene: Olivier-as-Hamlet, Jessica Tandy-as-Blanche, Joan MacIntosh-as-Mother Courage, Richard Chamberlain-as-Richard II. These agents are known for their ability to powerfully stimulate other actors fortunate enough to share scenes with them. Given that the moment-to-moment work of an actor is an ongoing give and take with others, then even the simple physical characteristics of another person, such as size, looks, and vocal quality, can help you experience inferiority, superiority, threat, anger, sexual attraction,* *and so on. Blue eyes can seem cool and cruel or bright and encouraging,* depending on what you need and how skillful you are at shaping and using what others offer you.

Environment (Setting). *The space where a scene occurs—a watchpost at Elsinore, a hot, sticky Southern tenement. Environments are immensely evocative. For example, at the beginning of* Dutchman, *Clay, a young black man, sits in a subway. The seat is moist with summer humidity and smells of stale air and cheap perfume. It is hard to swallow. The place next to Clay is empty, making him vulnerable to invasion by whomever the night should bring along. Shadows abound. The lighting is stark. Clay's eyes move to the only escape from his thoroughly uncomfortable surroundings—the window. Through this window he first sees Lula, the young white woman who becomes his seductress.*

Event (Personal Incident). *Whatever is happening to the character you are playing. For example, in* The Glass Menagerie, *there is a segment in which Amanda corrects her son's eating habits. If you are playing Tom, your statement of what is happening to you at that moment might be: "My mother is nagging me again." Toward the end of the play, Amanda discovers that the Gentleman Caller, Tom's friend, is engaged and cannot become the boyfriend she believes her daughter Laura needs. Amanda's sense of the event might be: "My son is making a fool of me." Accomplishing full, grounded contact with what is happening to you within the world of the play may be deeply disturbing or downright fun, but it is always arousing to an actor with the courage to confront and take in the personal incidents experienced by the character he or she is playing.*

In a sense, one of the most important services actors provide the rest of the human community (a. k. a. the audience) is to meet head-on those experiences the rest of us are afraid of, or which we desire but have not the resolution to embrace fully. Abandonment, rejection, denigrating relationships, and defeat are experiences in the first category, experiences through which we must all live. The second category might include falling in love, belonging, leaving home, or returning. These are poignant experiences that produce a strange blend of attraction and anxiety, springing perhaps from contradictory longings for both community and autonomy.

Time. *At least two kinds of time are important to an actor: time at which and time during. The first is exemplified by period, season, year—for instance, the spring of 1700, at the end of the Restoration period. The second refers to the amount and kind of time a character has and uses in a specific episode or plot event of a play. For example, the first meeting between Antigone and Ismene (in* Sophocles' Antigone*) often takes on a greater tension when both actors play as though they were being squeezed by the time limits on their conversation.*

Different actors plumb the given circumstances in different ways, searching for stimulation that is significant and appropriate. But many actors, early on in their preparation, try to generate as much material (as much provocative energy) as possible from each scene. As their work progresses, certain discoveries may become more useful than others. In the case of the actor playing Clay, the subway window may seem a more central part of the environment during the first few moments of the play, because it is through it that he sees Lula, his antagonist. This selection is a natural part of interpretation. Not everything in the given circumstances can remain equally important. But the best actors do not begin by limiting possibilities. Instead, they first try for as full a sense of situation as they can achieve.

In our workaday lives, we must often deal with situations in a way that diminishes their demands on us, but in the theatre we must do just the opposite. Working with the given circumstances means learning to invest them with the capacity to provoke reaction from us. If we are successful, acting becomes an ongoing, lively exchange with the world that surrounds us.

Introduction to the Given Circumstances:
Working with the Senses

The five senses are our primary means of making contact with the given circumstances, whether on or off the stage. Interaction between our senses and the world creates basic impressions (sensations), such as dark and light, hard and soft, high or low frequency, and so on. These impressions are important because they are the raw material from which we construct full-blown perceptual images (e.g., the sight of a sunrise, the taste of chili, the music of Mozart's *Requiem*, the feel of the summer heat). Therefore, before we begin working with each of the given circumstances individually, we will explore and revitalize our sensory and perceptual processes in preparation for the work to come in Chapters 5–9. As actors, what we get from sensing and perceiving is the heightened stimulation to respond readily and fully to whatever the given circumstances have to offer. Arrested, half-hearted, or invisible responses cannot sustain emotional life, energize the work of fellow actors, or affect an audience. To act effectively, our sensory and perceptual work must be more thorough and involving than the kind usually permitted by the hurly-burly of daily life. We must become connoisseurs of sensation and perception—whether it be the taste of Godiva chocolate, the smell of pizza, or the vision of morning "in russet mantle, clad."

Situations enclose us like caves and become the walls and ceilings of our concerns.
JOSEPH CHAIKIN,
THE PRESENCE OF THE ACTOR

CULTURAL TYRANNIES

Security, openness, and stillness (the subjects of Part I) are the preconditions for a more expansive style of sense perception and response, but there is lots more work to be done. Reawakening and developing our sensory and perceptual capacities means confronting a variety of cultural tyrannies that get in the way. One such tyranny stems from the endless number of simple categorical terms our culture affords us. Many of the labels we use—"tree," "car," "corner grocery"—serve as partial substitutes for sensory contact. To label something a "tree" means we do not have to attend to all the sensations (colors, smells, movements, sounds, and so on) that it offers. Once labeled, it can be shoved aside, and we can return to the comfortable din of our usual internal tape recordings. We need only enough sense data to trigger the appropriate label. Sensory involvement with the world is thus kept to a minimum. Efficient, yes; but also impoverishing.

Another tyranny comes from what some psychologists call "metaprograms." Broadly based on a variety of different kinds of social conditioning, a metaprogram is simply another, more complex labeling strategy. Often metaprograms work when there is some degree of uncertainty about what we are confronting. They bestow certainty by presenting us with pairs of either/or choices. For example, we may see something dimly in the distance. As we try to identify it our metaprograms start firing. Is it animate or inanimate? Animal or human? Male or female? Friendly or dangerous? Good or bad for us? And so on. The either/or choices usually zip by without our knowing it, leading us automatically to specific labels that are difficult to resist. The final label we choose becomes the actual program by which we decide how to respond to a specific perception. For example, after a long chain of either/or choices we arrive at the label "bad." This label is likely to determine how we feel and behave toward the object in question. Like the simple category labels, metaprograms are practical because they help us live our daily lives more easily. But also like category labels, metaprograms take a lot of the bang out of sense perception.

As actors, we may find both simple category labels and metaprograms interesting propositions, useful for understanding a character's values and preferences. The issue, however, is more fundamental—namely, reclaiming and amplifying our sensory and perceptual processes in a way that maximizes what we receive and take in from the given circumstances. The ways in which culture and socialization subvert a full use of sense perception do not give way easily to good intentions. Habits are difficult to change. We must go through a learning process before we can put off even some of the usual interventions of categories and metaprograms.

EXERCISES

The sensory and perceptual skills you learn in the exercises to come are crucial to your upcoming work with each of the given circumstances. So take your time. Let things happen rather than straining for the results you think are supposed to occur.

Prolonging and Multiplying Sense Perceptions

These first few exercises build on the work you have done with stillness. They are intended to rehearse you in a more vigorous use of your senses: first, by extending the time you remain in contact with a sense object; second, by multiplying the number of perceptions you acquire from the contact; and third, by allowing you to focus on one sense operation at a time.

Exercise 4–1: Seeing

1. Stand in front of a partner so you can look one another in the face.
2. Study each other's faces. Concentrate on detail.
3. Take turns reporting to one another everything each of you sees. Alternate so that your report takes the form of a dialogue. For example,

   A: I see a blotch on your glasses.

   B: I notice you smile when you talk.

   A: I notice you are wearing green earrings.

   B: I see your chin has a dimple.

   And so on.

4. Now, do the exercise again but without repeating anything you mentioned in your first report. Look for something new.

Exercise 4–2: Hearing

1. Stand back to back with your partner.
2. Repeat a brief line from a scene or poem several times, or simply say your names to one another a few times.
3. Then report everything you can recall about one another's voices (pitch, timbre, rate, inflection, pronunciation). Again, use dialogue form and talk to one another as in the previous exercise.
4. Repeat the exercise. Try to find and report vocal qualities you hadn't noticed the first time.

Exercise 4–3: Touching

1. Close your eyes and move your fingertips lightly over one another's hands for one minute.
2. Report in the form of a dialogue as many of the sensations as you can recall.
3. Once again, repeat the exercise looking for new sensations.

Exercise 4–4: Smell

1. Bring a flower or cup of coffee to class.
2. Create a dialogue in which you both report as many different characteristics of the odor as you can detect in one minute. Then repeat the exercise to discover new characteristics.

Exercise 4–5: Taste

1. Bring a small cookie or a piece of bread or fruit to class.
2. Chew it slowly. After swallowing it, report as many taste qualities as you can decipher.
3. Do the exercise again. See how many new qualities you find.

Sensation and Association

Sensations are bound up closely with our interior lives. What stimulates our senses stimulates the rest of our being as well.

Exercise 4–6: Visual Association Dialogue

1. Study your partner's face again.
2. Create a dialogue in which you both report whatever associations occur to you. For example,

   A: Your eyes *seem* warm.

   B: Your nose *reminds me* of how much I enjoyed the smell of that flower.

   A: Your chin *makes me think of* my father.

3. Words or phrases such as "seems," "reminds," or "makes me think of" are good ways to help yourself focus on your associations. So try to be honest and open to your own imagination and memory.
4. If you believe your associations will inhibit the other actor's work or embarrass you, simply say: "Go on." This means that you do not want to make a specific association part of the social field. Saying "go on"

when necessary is an important contribution to the work. Embarrassment does not promote good acting or help actors to work well together.

Exercise 4–7: Aural Association Dialogue

1. Listen to one another reciting a short poem, lines from a play, or one another's names.
2. Complete the exercise as above, focusing on the associations stimulated by one another's voices.

Exercise 4–8: Tactile Association Dialogue

1. Repeat the exercise exploring the backs of each other's hands with your fingers.

Exercise 4–9: Smell Association Dialogue

1. Base your associations on the odor of a flower, cup of coffee, tea, or an edible object.

Exercise 4–10: Taste Association Dialogue

1. Do the exercise one more time after tasting a bit of food.

Sensations and Impulses

Sensory experiences can create the tendency to do something, such as run, dance, laugh, scream, cry—that is, to engage in some overt, expressive behavior.

Exercise 4–11: Impulse Dialogue, Visual

1. Repeat the visual exercise given above.
2. But this time construct a dialogue in which you each report your impulses to one another. For example,

   A: I *want to stop* this exercise.

   B: I *want to stand* further away.

   A: I *need to quit* staring at your face.

   B: I'd *like to tickle* your nose.

3. Words and phrases such as "want to," "like to", and "need to" will help you make contact with your impulses. Moreover, it is not necessary to

explain why you are having the impulses that occur. Keep the dialogue simple. Respect yourself and your partner.

Exercise 4–12: Impulse Dialogue, Aural

1. Repeat the previous exercise, but this time focus on the impulses created by each other's voices.

Exercise 4–13: Impulse Dialogue, Tactile

1. Report the impulses that come with touching one another's hands.

Exercise 4–14: Impulse Dialogue, Taste

1. Report the impulses that occur as you drink a beverage.

Exercise 4–15: Impulse Dialogue, Smell

1. Report the impulses evoked by the smell of an edible substance.

Sensory Preference and Transference

Different individuals prefer certain senses over others, depending on the situation they find themselves in. Some may lead with their eyes when they drive a car, with taste and smell at the dinner table, or with their ears at a concert. Conversely, some senses are deemphasized in certain situations. The person who engages with his or her eyes while driving may make less use of smell and taste.

The senses we turn up or turn down are a matter of habit that may not always work to our advantage. If we turn up our senses of taste and smell at the dinner table but turn down our senses of sight and hearing, we may find it hard to interact successfully with others while eating. Those around us may find us inattentive and boorish. Similarly, a driver who turns up his eyes and ears but turns down his kinesthetic sense (touch) may become impervious to the feel of road conditions that come through the steering column. The exercises that follow are intended (1) to help you become aware of how you use your senses and (2) to show you some ways to expand your sense experience.

Exercise 4–16: Visual Transference

1. Find something in the room that has an appealing color. Study it closely

for a minute while breathing somewhat more slowly and deeply than normal.

2. Imagine how the color would sound.
3. How would it taste if it were food?
4. How would it smell?
5. How would the color feel if it touched the back of your neck?

Exercise 4–17: Aural Transference

1. Listen to a simple sound for about thirty seconds. It might be the humming of an appliance or a few pleasant notes sung or played on a musical instrument. Remember to keep your breathing relaxed.
2. If the sound were a color, what would it be? Try to see it.
3. If it had an odor, what scent would the sound give off?
4. Imagine the sound as a taste.
5. How would it feel on your hands if you could touch the sound?

Exercise 4–18: Smell Transference

1. Bring a flower or some other pleasant object to class. Enjoy its odor for about a minute.
2. Imagine the smell as a color. What would the color be?
3. How would the smell sound?
4. How would it taste?
5. What would it feel like on the back of your arms or on your legs?

Exercise 4–19: Taste Transference

1. Taste something you enjoy.
2. Imagine it as a color.
3. Then as a sound.
4. Next as a smell.
5. Then as a feeling on the tip of your nose.

Guidelines: Although these last four exercises may be done privately, you can enhance their results by working with a partner and sharing aloud what you experience. The exercises are easy to explain and do. But the results can be complex. If you feel dizzy, disoriented, or otherwise uncomfortable, you may be challenging your usual sensory preferences too rapidly. Stop for a moment. Then begin working more slowly.

Body/Emotion/Sensation

The focus of the next set of exercises is the way emotions create sensations in the body by being connected to muscular activity. Work through the exercises three or four times, in order to get the hang of them slowly. Keep your work leisurely but well focused on what you are doing in each step.

Exercise 4–20: Emotion as Sensation

1. Stand or sit in a relaxed but upright position.
2. Breathe a bit more slowly and deeply than normal. Be careful not to hyperventilate.
3. Take a minute to identify your dominant emotional state. You need not fish for anything grand. If it's Friday, you may feel mildly "up"; on a Monday, a bit "down." Use a simple label for how you feel. If you are uncertain, just take a guess.
4. Try to discover where the emotion "lives" in your body. Maybe you feel the mild "up" of a Friday as a lightness in your chest, or the nagging dread of a Monday as a coffee-queasiness in the pit of your stomach.
5. Breathe deeply but easily into that part of your body. Hold your breath for four or five seconds (a short time); then exhale, releasing and loosening the muscles in that particular area.
6. Repeat the previous step three or four times. Observe what happens to your feelings. They may change or remain the same. Perhaps they become more or less intense. There is no single right result.

Exercise 4–21: Adding the Voice

1. Once again, identify and label your overall emotional state. (Remember to breathe with a relaxed torso.)
2. Find the muscle group associated with the feeling.
3. Also find a simple sound (not a word) that you think expresses the feeling (e.g., maybe a groan for the Monday yucks or a "yeah" for the Friday ups).
4. Exhale freely, releasing the muscle group and uttering the sound you have chosen.
5. Repeat step 4 three or four times. Pay attention to whatever happens—to changes or similarities in your emotional states. Once again, you are not working for any one result.

Exercise 4–22: Incorporating Larger Movements

1. Again, identify whatever emotion seems to be most prominent. (Don't hurry. Relax and go with the first feeling you are aware of.)

2. Decide what muscle structure seems to be holding the feeling.

3. Find a simple movement (the larger the better without straining) that activates those particular muscles. Repeat the movement several times, allowing it to carry through the rest of your body. Make sure your breathing remains relaxed and a trifle slower than usual.

4. After a minute of movement, join your voice to the exercise, using the sound that feels right (one that makes the movement easier or more fluid).

5. Observe whatever changes occur.

How did a set of exercises dealing with emotion get into work on sense perception? The exercises suggest that emotions are closely associated with our bodies. With a little concentration, we learn to feel them as body states (in spite of the metaprograms that get in the way). This means that our emotions take on a physical presence in the form of sensations (such as heaviness, lightness, muscle tension, tingling, numbness, and so on). Our awareness of these sensations comes to us through tactile contact with our own bodies. (We can feel our bodies move, hold, tingle, or go numb.) The body is both part of self and part of the world—the site from which we make sensory contact with other objects and at the same time one of the objects of that contact. To truly "get in touch" with the world is to make contact with the self and vice versa.

Haikus in Sound and Motion[1]

Writing haikus is one of the best ways to make yourself aware of the relationship among perception, the body, and your inner life. Haikus are seventeen-syllable poems, divided into three lines of five, seven, and five. For purposes of the exercises in this section, start with a specific sense impression or complete perception, then let it stimulate associations, impulses, or emotional states. You need not work all three into your verse.

Here are two examples to get you started:

The smell of coffee—
The snap, crackle, pop of kids:
Saturday morning.
                    J. G.-T.

The wind ices my beard.
Inside, children and a fire:
My face thaws with smiles.
                    J. G.-T.

Writing a haiku is just the beginning. For a poet the movement from impression to full expression may find completion in the written word. But for an actor, expression is not complete until it becomes embodied.

Exercise 4–23: Sound and Motion Improvisation

1. Write a haiku, as described above.

2. Say it aloud six to ten times, experimenting with different speeds and volumes.

3. Now, begin moving as you say the haiku. No need to act your poem out. Just move to it as though the words were music. The process is one of discovery. You are not supposed to know what moves will feel right ahead of time. Just let the movement come as you speak your lines.

4. Continue the movement for five to ten minutes. Vary the size, rhythm, and intensity of your work.

5. Observe whatever occurs by way of physical sensations, associations, impulses, or emotional states.

Guidelines: There is no right or wrong. The only goal is to sensitize yourself to whatever you are experiencing from moment to moment.

Together, the words, movements, body sensations, associations, impulses, and/or feelings—in whatever combination—constitute the experience you are having. All the awarenesses that make up your experience are important. On stage and in the studio, trying to blot out your awarenesses is constricting and self-defeating. Instead, allow yourself to focus on whatever the work brings on.

I have staged this chapter as a journey inward from simple sense perception to emotion. The body has been a constant throughout this journey—a means to a more ample sensory life and to more vivid inner awareness. Body states are part of all our experiences (not necessarily a cause [James and Lange] or an effect [Strasberg and so many others], but a fundamental part). The body is an environment that makes possible all of the processes of being human. Without it, experience would have no way of forming. In this sense, the body is like a theatre where all sorts of things happen and which is, at the same time, actively involved in all the happenings.

If experience is corporeal, why hold on to words like *inner* and *outer, physical,* and *psychological?* We do so because these words help us select and focus on specific aspects of our overall experience—on different happenings within the "theatre." If I am especially happy, I may want language that will call attention to this fact without at the same time bringing attention to my broken foot. But words that help us be specific in a conversation are only conveniences. They spring from our need to communicate intelligibly with others. Words like *internal* and *external, intellectual* and *emotional* do not deny that experience is embodied but only attest to the complexity of communicating our experiences to others. The problem with language habits is that sometimes they hide certain sorts of awarenesses from us. One of the goals of this chapter, and of this book for that matter, is to help you achieve a sense of yourself that goes beyond the boundaries of everyday language.

The actor is a person involved in the age-old quest for freedom from the constraints of society and culture. But the actor's approach is unique. Instead of fleeing the world for the solitude of the mountain, the desert, or the cave, he or she actively seeks a more total engagement with the world. Ironically, in the theatre, freedom comes not from flight but from whole, personal investment. On stage as in the circus, if we would fly, we must learn how to give ourselves completely to our surroundings.

NOTES

1. I owe the idea for this lesson to William Kuhlke.

REFERENCES

Chaikin, Joseph. *The Presence of the Actor.* New York: Atheneum, 1972.

James, Tad, and Wyatt Woodsmall. *Time Line Therapy and the Basis of Personality.* Cupertino, CA: Meta Publications, 1988. Among other things, the authors fully describe metaprograms and how they relate to values and daily psychological behavior.

Lankton, Steven. *Practical Magic.* Cupertino, CA: Meta Publications, 1980. The book is a beginning manual for neurolinguistic programming. Although written for therapists, it offers a number of concepts particularly useful for acting. My own thinking about sensory preference and transference was stimulated, in part, by Lankton's first four chapters.

Rizzo, Raymond. *The Total Actor.* Indianapolis, IN: Bobbs-Merrill, 1975. Read Chapter 6 for an approach to the given circumstanccs that combines Stanislavski with a tinge of yoga.

Stanislavski, Constantin. *An Actor Prepares.* Translated by Elizabeth Reynolds Hapgood. New York: Theatre Arts Books, 1977 [first copyright, 1936]. See Chapters 3 to 5.

———. *Creating a Role.* Translated by Elizabeth Reynolds Hapgood. New York: Theatre Arts Books, 1968 [third printing; first copyright 1961]. Pages 12 through 34 provide one portion of Stanislavski's approach to the given circumstances. Another part is given in *An Actor Prepares.*

*(Notes, ideas,
sketches, reactions
to the exercises . . .)*

(Notes, ideas,
sketches, reactions
to the exercises . . .)

(Notes, ideas,
sketches, reactions
to the exercises . . .)

_____

_____

_____

_____

_____

_____

_____

_____

_____

_____

_____

_____

_____

_____

_____

_____

_____

_____

Working with Others

An actor's interaction with others on stage revolves around the notion of contact. Contact depends and builds upon everything studied in Part I. In its initial stages, though, contact probably relies most especially on openness (see Chapter 2). Human contact begins when the participants in an interaction open themselves up to mutual influence. The more open to influence each is, the fuller the contact. In the context of the theatre, openness to influence really means the willingness to change from one moment to the next in response to whatever the other actor is doing. Contact is the lifeblood of mutual adjustment. Genuine connection with another human being makes it impossible for actors to stay on one level of feeling or expression.

The idea of contact frames acting as a true exchange of energy and impact by which actors help create one another's work. In fact, the reason why other actors/characters are called agents within the given circumstances is because they are instrumental in creating your performance. There is nothing more useless than actors who pump themselves up with whatever feelings or energy they think a scene requires of them. The result is a black hole in the stage space—a void made up of gobs of activity but with no transference of energy. On stage, energy never comes from the self alone but always from contact with another.

Contact is risky business. It is sometimes easy for inexperienced actors to confuse a sense of contact with the sort of generic good feelings

Through contact, each person has the chance to meet the world outside himself nourishingly.
ERVING AND
MIRIAM POLSTER,
*GESTALT THERAPY
INTEGRATED*

[O]nce contact is made it is the same for all; a charge of excitement exists within the individ-ual which culmi-nates in a sense of full engagement with whatever is interesting at that moment.

ERVING AND
MIRIAM POLSTER

associated with campfires, pep rallies, and some forms of group therapy. What distinguishes mature contact from merely being together and liking it is a sense of boundary that preserves the separateness and integrity of each actor. The contact that is most useful on stage is a meeting of separate individuals, none of whom have sacrificed any personal power for the sake of social harmony, who open themselves to change and adjustment not out of insecurity or a need for acceptance but with self-confidence and a sense of personal worth. *Contact becomes theatrically charged when actors meet one another head-on, with their capacity to influence and provoke adjustment in full force. Otherwise, there is no true give-and-take but only social accommodation.*

A clear image of the sort of contact that is crucial on stage comes from the following experiment in family dynamics. Researchers gave married couples pillows and asked them to fight. Those who had the healthiest marriages hit each other harder and more frequently than couples in crisis or on the verge of divorce. Mature contact—pillow-to-pillow, body-to-body, mind-to-mind, self-to-self—is a no-holds-barred exchange of strate-gic differences that is nonetheless deep and supportive. A strategic differ-ence is a unique quality in one actor that brings out a unique quality in the other. These strategic differences are expressed as powerful, moment-to-moment adjustments, stimulated by the presence of other actors and directed back at them—like a fight between lovers.

Since lots of dramatic characters live in relationships gone to ruin, an audience might convince itself that poor connective work on the part of the actors is really a problem of the characters. But in performance, the best actors (no matter how skewed the relationship between the characters they play) are always telling us something about human community. For example, selfish, nonconnective acting can do no more than create a sense of pity for the characters in the disintegrating Wingfield family (in *The Glass Menagerie*). But truly reciprocal acting brings the audience beyond pity by instilling a sense of poignancy and a longing for precisely what the Wingfields cannot attain: communion. The deep mutuality that character-izes vibrant contact moves an audience beyond the predicament of the characters they are watching and reminds them of the fragility, value, and power of the human bond—no matter how shattered or distorted that bond may be within the fictional world of the play.

As an actor, contact must become one of your subcultural habits and a constant part of your presence on stage. Great actors know how to relate to one another directly and immediately. Through training and experi-ence, they have become generous enough to give both powerfully and selflessly, and humble enough to receive what is given in return. When it comes to working with others on stage, craft becomes ethics and ethics becomes a rigorous craft.

EXERCISES

Warming Up to Contact

Seeing, hearing, and touching are social instruments. You use them to make and break off contact. They can help you reach out or seal yourself off from others. Since you use them in your social lives, seeing, hearing, and touching make a good place to begin your work with others.

Exercise 5–1: Eye Contact

1. For this exercise, you and a partner will need to memorize a dialogue. There are short "jumps" and longer scenes in the appendix. You will be coming back to this dialogue from time to time throughout the chapter.

2. Sit or stand eight to ten feet away from your partner and make eye contact. Try to stay focused outwardly. Notice as many details about the other person's eyes as you can. Observe when you break off contact and when you come back. Do not turn the exercise into a staring contest or force yourself to maintain eye contact.

3. After a minute, begin exchanging lines from your memorized dialogue while maintaining your concentration on one another's eyes.

4. Allow the lines to come slowly at first. Then gradually, permit the dialogue to become fluid. It can be repeated for as long as you wish the exercise to last.

Guidelines: The purpose of steps 3 and 4 is to help you transfer the enhanced contact from the earlier steps to the text. If your concentration is as pure as it is supposed to be, you might not know if the transfer is occurring. Consult with your instructor. If the transference is not full enough, go back to step 1 and move more gradually to step 4.

Exercise 5–2: Eye Contact, at the Close Boundary

1. Walk toward your partner until you begin to feel a bit uncomfortable; then take one step back into your comfort range.

2. Find a social posture you use every day: sit in a chair with one leg crossed over the other or stand with your weight on one leg and your arms crossed. Choose something easy and simple.

3. Now, repeat the previous exercise.

Exercise 5–3: Connecting by Ear I

1. Start telling your partner the story of your day—what time you got up, what you had for breakfast—the more mundane the better.

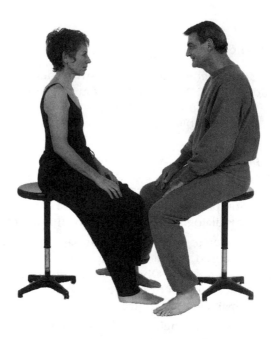

EYE CONTACT, AT THE
CLOSE BOUNDARY,
STEP 2.
Keep the contact simple.
There is no need to do
anything dramatic. Just
look at one another.

2. After twenty or thirty seconds, stop and let your partner start the story of his or her day. He or she must begin on the same pitch as you left off on.

3. Continue the exercise for two to five minutes, switching back and forth at twenty- to thirty-second intervals.

Exercise 5–4: Connecting by Ear II

1. Repeat the previous exercise.

2. However, now when it comes time to switch speakers, start on a pitch opposite that of your partner's last word; for example, if your partner ends high, you should begin low or vice versa. (Remember to use normal, conversational voices.)

Exercise 5–5: Connecting by Ear III

1. Have your partner start the story of a recent episode of his or her life. The simpler the story the better.

2. After a brief time, cut in and begin your own story, trying to reproduce your partner's vocal manner for a couple of sentences. Then gradually return to your own natural inflections.

3. Avoid working for laughs and let each turn last about one minute.

The last three exercises are not really about pitch or vocal quality at all. They are about listening. Listening intently to another human being means listening to or for something specific. Moreover, the more concrete this "something" is, the more attentive and focused the listening can be. For example, listening for a final pitch or a characteristic vocal quality (inflection, rhythm, and so on) is more concrete than listening for an abstract "meaning." While these last few exercises made their way around the class, you may have noticed the physical changes that people made in order to hear specific vocal characteristics. Listening as an actor must listen is a physical process, one that requires adjustments from the entire body.

Besides pitch, rhythm, and inflection patterns, there can be other targets for your listening. You might try to hear when your partner takes a breath or notice on which words she or he makes a major change in eye contact. The best kind of listening engages you in the moment-to-moment behaviors of the other actors. Moreover, this kind of engagement is what allows them to have an impact on your ongoing process of physical and mental changes.

Transferring Physical Contact

The next three exercises continue the sensory transference work begun in the last chapter. On stage, seeing and listening are more usual modes of contact than touching. Yet touching has a great deal of impact. The purpose of the following exercises is to transfer the impact of physical contact with other human beings to your experience of seeing and hearing them.

Exercise 5–6: Tactile Connections I

1. Sit or stand facing your partner. Make eye contact.
2. Hold hands and do the dialogue you have memorized.
3. Squeeze or press your partner's hands on the words you think are particularly important. Be gentle.
4. After repeating the dialogue three to five times, let go of one another's hands and repeat it without touching one another.

Exercise 5–7: Tactile Connections II

1. Sit on the floor back to back.
2. Lean against one another comfortably.
3. Repeat the dialogue three to five times. Alter the pressure against your partner's back in accord with the words you want to stress.
4. Then move apart and face each other. Make eye contact and go through the dialogue three or four more times.

Exercise 5–8: Tactile Connections III

1. Sit in chairs or on the floor facing one another.

2. Make eye contact. Hold hands and make sure your knees are touching.

3. Repeat the dialogue four or five times.

4. As you speak to one another, maintain eye contact, but move apart gradually, until you are not touching. Repeat the dialogue another three or four times after you have separated.

Mutual Adjustment Exercises

On stage, the communication between actors is like a dance. Together they engage in a dynamic exchange of kinesthetic adjustments (movements) that are shaped by and actually help to shape their inner lives. Even speaking, when it is done well, involves the whole body and is therefore part of the larger "dance" by which actors make contact. The "dance" of a trained actor is supposed to be a special medium of intimacy—penetrating, responsive, and full-bodied enough to make the audience feel and participate in the connections on stage.

Using the image of a dance, the next exercises will help you develop a more physical sense of the communication process. You are under no obligation to make your work entertaining to anyone. Trying to concoct a performance or worrying about the impression you are making are ways of isolating yourself and abandoning your partner. A basic rule of acting is "never leave your partner alone."

Exercise 5–9: Warmth Dance

1. Stand close enough so that you and your partner can feel the warmth from one another's hands, faces, necks, and heads.

2. Move continuously but without losing contact with the sensation of warmth.

3. Focus on the warmth and on whatever associations, impulses, and feelings may occur.

Guidelines: Here the dance is slow; the movement concentrated.

Exercise 5–10: Warmth Dance with Voice

1. Repeat the previous exercise. After a minute, incorporate your dialogue. Once again the body work should lead the vocal work.

2. Continue the exercise for three to five minutes. Then begin reducing the physical work until you and your partner are facing one another.

WARMTH DANCE.
The point of concentration throughout the exercise is the warmth emanating from your partner's skin.

ENERGY DANCE.
Remember, you must
both give *and* take
energy.

3. Do the dialogue three or four more times. Concentrate on the other actor; allow adjustments to occur as they will.

Exercise 5–11: Energy Dance

1. You and your partner are standing up to your waists in a pool of energy. (Imagine it however you wish: a pool of water, champagne, or cola bubbles, light beams of all colors. Use an image you find inviting.)

2. Move around vigorously and splash energy all over each other, letting your energy build and become more exuberant. But work gradually; do not use it all up in the first minute.

3. Make sure to keep moving as much as possible but remain close enough for the image of "splashing" to make sense.

4. Pay attention to the feelings, associations, and so on that occur as you work.

Guidelines: This dance is up-tempo and exuberant.

ENERGY DANCE, *continued.*

Exercise 5–12: Voice and Energy Dance

1. Repeat the exercise.
2. Work for about a minute; then add the dialogue you've been working with.
3. As always, let your voice be a by-product of your muscular activity and movement.
4. Gradually let the movement fall away, until you are facing one another in normal alignment. Allow gestures and adjustments to occur as they will.

Exercise 5–13: Adjustment Sequence

1. Stand at a comfortable distance from your partner.
2. Take a moment to establish eye contact.
3. Begin moving in relationship to one another without stopping. Let the movement be as free and expressive as possible.
4. Focus on the other person rather than on trying to plan what you are going to do next.
5. Try to create a "flow," moving continually in relation to your partner's movement.

Guidelines: There are no right or wrong movements, but there are some useful strategies: (1) Don't touch one another. (2) Concentrate on the other person, not on your own activities. (3) Think of your movement as triggering or evoking the other person's movements. Think of your partner's as triggering yours. (4) Avoid "making deals" with one another. There is no need to establish a movement pattern that can be repeated over and over again. Let each movement be different.

Exercise 5–14: Including the Voice

1. You can expand the last exercise by adding vocal work.
2. Move in relationship to one another for a minute or two. Then begin the dialogue you have memorized.[1]
3. After three to five minutes, start reducing the physical work gradually, until you are facing one another, standing in a normal posture.
4. Repeat the dialogue two or three more times, without trying to do anything specific with your body or voice. Just relax and concentrate on one another.

Exercise 5–15: Physical Analogies

1. Find a physical relationship with your partner that seems to summarize or capture the relationship between the characters in the dialogue you've been using.

2. Keep it simple. For example, you might decide to face in opposite directions, or stand "miles" apart. Perhaps one of you will want to stand on a chair or bench while the other kneels on the floor. Your choice of a physical analogy should spring from an overall impression of the scene or jump—that is, from the sense you make by reading and re-reading it.

3. Once you have discovered a physical analogy for your relationship in the script, speak your lines while focusing on the sensations, feelings, and/or associations that accompany the physical work.

4. After repeating the dialogue a few times, reduce the physical analogy by increments until you are facing one another in normal physical postures.

5. Repeat the dialogue two or three more times; relax and concentrate on one another. Let your voice and body go.

The last seven exercises add detail to the notion of human experience as a physical event. It is not merely the body that is the substratum and occasion for experience but more specifically the body's motility (that is, its flexibility, malleability, and suppleness) that determines its ability to form and re-form in response to various stimuli. Social norms that inhibit the body's reactive motion also mute the vividness of the sensations, perceptions, impulses, and memories that help to compose our experiences.

Exercising the Three R's

Contact with one another is a process. First, there is a moment of organic expansion and excitation, which comes as a result of *receiving* stimuli and impressions from the other actor. Second, we *reorganize* to ready ourselves to "ex-press" the energy that has been received. This reorganizing stage is a transition that prepares us on all levels to react to what we are taking in. The third stage is *returning* energy back to our partner in an attempt to act upon the world—either to encourage more of what we are receiving or to alter it in some way.

Receiving, reorganizing, and *returning* form a natural pulsation that structures our moment-to-moment connections with others. The pulsation is unconscious and involuntary. But it often becomes distorted. Many of us emphasize one phase over another, as in the following examples.

Some actors are best at receiving a charge from their surroundings. They always appear very full on stage, and their experience in each moment may run very deeply. But they are weak on the return. Their expressive work is often cliché-ridden or tentative. They seem more powerful when they are listening than when they speak. While their presence on stage promises much, it delivers less. Reorganizers, on the other hand, are often out of rhythm with other actors, as though they have stumbled into the wrong production. Teachers and directors accuse them of "overintellectualizing." But reorganizers are not always really thinking. It is just that they have an internal process that has come detached from receiving and returning. They often look stuck, as though they do not know what to do next. Finally, actors who prefer only to put energy into their surroundings come off distorted in another way. It is very difficult to give what you have not got. So, the work of these actors seems strident, squeezed, overblown, and contrived. They are always manufacturing their own energy instead of receiving it from outside themselves. These are the kinds of actors who look at your forehead instead of your eyes, or throw their eyes out of focus so nothing gets in.

These three examples are really cartoons meant to illustrate a point. Although none of us may have interpersonal processes that are misshapen enough to produce the exaggerated oral, schizoid, or retentive "symptoms" I have just sketched, all of us are liable to some degree of distortion in the basic pulsation of our contact with others. This is a natural consequence of the pressures of life and the anxiety that often accompanies coming on stage into public view.

The following exercises will help you make the movement from receiving to reorganizing to returning clearer and more well-proportioned.

Exercise 5–16: What? Exchange, Visual and Aural

1. Look at your partner.
2. Wait until you get a definite impression. The impression can be a certain feeling, a felt need to communicate, discomfort with the silence, or a desire to get on with it—just about any impression will work.
3. When your impression (no matter what it is) comes into focus, ask the question "What?" as though your partner had said something you didn't quite hear. Your partner should answer, "I said 'hello.' "
4. Build a dialogue on this exchange. Every two or three minutes switch parts.

Guidelines: Stay focused on your partner. You don't have to be able to name the impression (feeling or impulse) you are getting. If you find yourself waiting between lines, you may be working for too big a charge. Breathe easily and take what comes.

Exercise 5–17: What? Exchange, Tactile

1. Repeat the exercise holding hands.
2. Then with your knees touching.
3. Finally, repeat it sitting back to back.

Guidelines: Repeat the dialogue several times. Spending four or five minutes on each step is fine.

Exercise 5–18: Coming Back to the Text

1. Now stand or sit facing one another but without touching.

2. Go through the dialogue you memorized at the beginning of the exercises in this chapter. Concentrate on one another without worrying about carrying anything over from the exercise.

Exercise 5–19: Who? Exchange, Visual and Aural

1. Look at one another in silence until one of you gets a definite impression.

2. But instead of using "What?" as the trigger question, use "Who?" The dialogue sequence is also a little different:

   A: Who?

   B: I said my name is _____ . (Use your own or the name of the character you are playing.)

3. After you have repeated the exchange several times, switch lines with your partner. Stick to the dialogue as written.

Exercise 5–20: Who? Exchange, Tactile

1. Repeat the exercise holding hands.

2. Then do so with knees touching.

3. Finally, repeat it sitting back to back.

Exercise 5–21: Coming Back to the Text

1. Face one another sitting or standing.

2. Concentrate on one another without feeling obligated to repeat what you got from the exercises.

3. Talk to one another using the words of your memorized dialogue.

Contact Support

The next group of exercises emphasizes giving and taking support—a skill crucial to your work with one another. On stage you are responsible for the other actors' work and they are responsible for yours. "Taking care of yourself" on stage is a one-way street to a dead performance. This is a good time to recall a point begun in Part I: For energy to be expressive, it must be "extra-verted," other directed.

Exercise 5–22: Back to Back, Head to Head

1. Stand in the middle of the acting space with a partner.

2. Begin by leaning against one another, back to back. Make sure you are supporting the other person's weight *and at the same time* letting him or her support yours. Throughout the exercise, you must give and take support *simultaneously.*

3. Move continuously but slowly from one supportive physical connection to another, as illustrated in the photographs. There is no need to plan the moves ahead of time. Just improvise.

4. Take your time.

Guidelines: Work on a mat to take some of the fear out of leaning and being leaned on. You might discover that you prefer to give rather than accept support or vice versa. Your preferences may indicate what it takes for you to feel safe and in control on stage. Balancing your willingness to give and receive support is an ideal. The fact that you may not achieve the balance on the first try means only that you are human.

Exercise 5–23: Support with Words

1. Repeat the exercise, starting in the back-to-back position. Concentrate on the bodily sensations that come from supporting and being supported.

2. After a minute, begin a dialogue made up only of the word *yes.*

3. Trade this word back and forth without inhibiting or stopping your physical work. Observe the simple rule that whenever your partner says yes, you must respond in kind.

4. The word *yes* coupled with the direct physical contact is bound to stimulate feelings. Simply notice the feelings that occur while you are working. They are not separate from the work but part of it.

5. Think of your feelings as the energy that comes from and goes back into the supportive exchange with the other actor.

Exercise 5–24: Back to the Text

1. Once again, begin back to back.

2. Work for about a minute or until the movement from one supportive position to another occurs fluidly.

3. Then begin the dialogue you memorized earlier in this chapter.

4. Let your voice (tone, pitch, pace, and so on) come out of contact and movement.

BACK TO BACK, HEAD TO HEAD.
After beginning this exercise back to back, try to discover supportive positions spontaneously rather than planning them ahead of time. Let your movements flow from one to another.

Guidelines: Avoid trying to do anything special with the lines. Focus hard on how the physical contact and movement feel. Let the lines come by the way, as though produced by the exercise.

The support exercises are a commanding metaphor for your work with others, whether on stage or in the studio. Everything you do is done *with, for,* and *to* one another—all three at the same time. Each of you molds and sustains the responses of the other according to rules of engagement contained in the exercise, and each of you is supposed to get as much as you give. The more dynamic the exchanges of support, the more fluid and adventuresome the movement becomes. Your impact on one another is not just physical. Supportive contact excites your interior life. Feelings come out of the corner of your eye, as it were, without your having to work for them. How can you not have feelings about body-to-body work with another human being? All your feelings are right as long as you let the rules shape how they influence your work. Self-indulgence begins when you let your feelings destroy the rules of the game, exercise, or production.

Remembering Others

One way the presence of another person can have an impact is by reminding us of someone from our past. The feelings from the past relationship transfer to the present and become part of our overall emotional response to the person with whom we are actually dealing. This transfer of affect from a past to a present other is not always conscious. In fact, it is a more or less normal activity that goes on unconsciously throughout the many interactions that make up our day. Part of the way we feel when we talk to neighbors, friends, colleagues, or the postman comes from the fact that they remind us of someone else.

But memories are not just mental artifacts. They are stored in the body as complex muscular formations originally begun in response to the impact of another. Our bodies bear the imprints of significant relationships we have had with our mothers, fathers, siblings, teachers, lovers, friends, and enemies. Equally important is that these physical residues from past relationships function as the "storehouses" of the feelings that were also part of those relationships. Someone who reminds us of a former lover triggers an entire psychophysical organization—a web of small and large physical and emotional responses that were originally formed in a relationship we had once upon a time.

The strategies of suppression (muscular armor, internal noise, and so on) are often part of our unconscious efforts to simplify our present relationships by keeping memory under wraps, as it were—to keep it from becoming too emotionally powerful and threatening our social "cool." None of us wants the past to overwhelm the present. But on stage the wellspring of feelings that comes from remembered relationships can contribute power and emotional range to our contact with others—if we are willing to put aside our defenses and embrace our pasts *in a carefully structured way that allows us to control what the memories do.*

There are two notions to keep in mind during the exercises that follow. First, all the mnemonic work you do is intended to predispose you to react more personally and deeply to your fellow actors. The specific aim of the exercises is to help you transfer feelings about others from your past to the person you are working with, so he or she will be able to get to you. Second, although simple, the physical portion of each exercise is nonetheless important. Reading the instructions for each exercise before beginning will help you avoid breaking concentration or interrupting the rhythm of your work.

Exercise 5–25: You Remind Me of . . .

1. Look at your partner until you find some characteristic that reminds you of someone from your past.

2. Tell your partner as simply as possible what about him or her reminds you of the other. Then tell your partner something about the person you are remembering: For example, "Your hair reminds me of my uncle. He used to pat me on the back and call me buddy." Or, "My brother used to wear shoes like yours. Now, he lives in Spokane and has five kids." (Watch out for those shoes.)

3. Construct a dialogue with your partner in which you share the simple, upbeat memories that each of you triggers in the other.

4. Impasse occurs when one or both of you can find no further memories in one another, or when the memories you can find are no longer upbeat. At that point, change partners.

Exercise 5–26: Physicalizing Memory

1. Look at a new partner until you are reminded of someone from your past.

2. Do not vent the memory by relating it out loud as before.

3. Instead, find a simple physical position or activity that captures/clarifies some aspect of the relationship you had with the person you are remembering: For example, perhaps you will shake hands with your partner, or lock arms as though to dance, or stand shoulder to shoulder in a position of mutual support and defense. Make sure your breathing remains relaxed and deep.

4. Prolong the physical analogy you have chosen while you repeat your jump or scene two to four times. Then let your partner choose a memory and a physical analogy.

Guidelines: This can be powerful stuff. What happens if one or both of you cannot relax enough to breathe freely? Choose a different memory or analogy, something less intense or more upbeat.

Exercise 5–27: Somatic Memory

1. Observe your partner from head to toe until you are reminded of someone you know or knew.

2. Share with your partner a very short memory about the person. Again focus on something simple: For example, "You remind me of a childhood friend. I can remember the time my friend and I went to the store and the clerk gave us free bubblegum."

3. After telling the story, take a moment to become aware of how you feel about the memory right now. (If you find that your dominant feeling is nervousness at having others listening to you, that's O.K. Go with it.)

4. Now discover the muscle group where the feeling seems to reside.

5. Breathe into and out of those muscles a few times and relax as you exhale.

6. Repeat your original memorized dialogue three to five times. As you do so, focus your concentration more and more on your partner. *The more unconscious the memory becomes at this point the better.* Free yourself of any concern for getting the "right" results.

7. Now assist your partner in doing the exercise.

Exercise 5–28: Memory in Motion

1. Repeat the last exercise.

2. After you breathe into the muscle group most involved with your memory, begin to move in a way that activates those muscles. The only purpose of the movement is to set certain muscles in motion. You are not required to demonstrate or act out anything.

3. After two or three minutes of movement, begin your memorized dialogue.

4. Repeat it four or five times, gradually reducing the size of the motion until it disappears, and you are eventually standing facing your partner at a comfortable distance.

5. Repeat the dialogue one or two more times without worrying about carryover. Place your attention fully on your partner.

6. Change places with your partner and repeat the exercise.

The last sequence of exercises required you to make a very brief subtext in the form of a personal story from your past. Typically, a subtext is whatever the actor/character is thinking or feeling. It is "sub" because it is unspoken in performance and works "underneath" the text to influence the emotional tone of the spoken dialogue by making the words personal for the actor.

However, the subtexts in the last three exercises are composed not only of a story about a remembered other but also of muscular activity associated with the memory. The moving body is part of the subtext and helps it to become deeply felt rather than a mere constellation of words.

Exercise 5–29: Mother and Father

1. With your partner, run the dialogue you have been using.

2. Inject the word *mother, father, mom,* or *dad* somewhere in each of your lines as though you were addressing them directly to your parents.

3. Repeat the exercise with your partner until the dialogue becomes fluid. Make sure to breathe freely and easily.

Mother and *father* are words that do more than trigger particular mental pictures. The labels touch off entire psychophysical organizations (muscular formations plus feelings). In other words, each of us has a way of organizing ourselves when we think of our parents. This organization is the beginning of our response to their memory. Calling other actors "mother" or "father" empowers them to evoke in us the psychophysical organizations we have associated with these words.

Exercise: 5–30: Mother and Father as Somatic Forms

1. Do your memorized dialogue with a partner, injecting the word *mother* or *father* in each passage as you did in the preceding exercise.

2. Notice what feelings occur and what muscle groups seem involved with the feelings.

3. Now, repeat the dialogue one or two more times. Before each of your lines, take a moment to inhale into the muscle group.

4. As you speak, imagine you are letting go and loosening that muscle group.

5. Repeat the dialogue two or three times. Concentrate on your partner and let the carryover from the exercise occur without any special effort on your part.

Guidelines: You may find that lots of muscles are associated with your feelings. Pick just one specific group. You can repeat the exercise a few times to work with the other muscles that are involved.

Exercise 5–31: Feeling and Movement

1. Repeat the exercise.

2. Locate the muscle groups where your feelings seem to "live." Then activate the muscles with large movements.

3. As you and your partner move, begin exchanging lines from your dialogue.

4. Gradually decrease the amount of movement until you are standing in one place facing one another. Allow your body to function normally. Continue the dialogue one or two more times. Again, forget the exercise and trust that your work has had impact.

Role Games

A single actor usually plays one character. But in many cases, that character enacts several roles at different times. The actor playing Hamlet, for example, functions as "son," "friend," "soldier," "nut," "wimp," "bully," "smart-ass," "confused child," "hero," and so on. To play the position of Hamlet in the game called *Hamlet* requires the actor to play all the roles Hamlet uses in order to get what he wants. But more important for this chapter, to share a scene with the actor playing Hamlet, you must focus on and experience whatever in the other actor's behavior is wimpy, bullyish, friendly, nuts, childish, and so on. That is, you must react to the way the other plays the game just as he or she must react to the way you play. The following exercises are intended to help you see, hear, feel, and respond to the role behaviors of your fellow actors.

Exercise 5–32: Role Definition

1. With a partner, choose roles by using one of the two diagrams. Each of you plays a role at one end or the other of the same arrow. Each role has a short piece of dialogue assigned to it. Repeat it throughout the exercise.

2. In order to make your own role clear, vivid, and stimulating for your partner, begin by exaggerating it as much as possible. As you repeat the role game (15–20 times), gradually make your behaviors smaller and more normal.

3. After you've completed the exercise, tell one another what behaviors (movements, gestures, voice qualities, facial expressions, and so on) you each found most evocative and stimulating—most useful for helping you play your own assigned role.

Guidelines: It may take a few moments for you to find the sorts of behaviors that go with your assigned role. But if you keep your work simple, you can begin to forget yourself and concentrate on your partner. Experiencing *your partner's* role behaviors is the focus of the exercise.

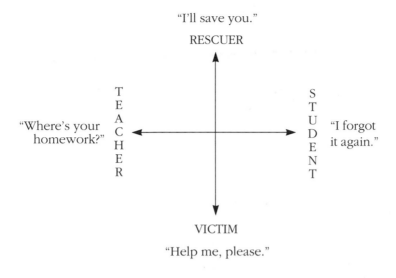

"I'll save you."

RESCUER

TEACHER "Where's your homework?"

STUDENT "I forgot it again."

VICTIM

"Help me, please."

"Be home on time."

PARENT

MASTER "Where are my shoes?"

SLAVE "Coming right up, your majesty."

CHILD

"I'm old enough to stay out."

Out of context the quote in the margin may seem glib. But it emphasizes the principle mentioned in the introduction to the last exercise. Roles elicit roles. Your own role behaviors are part of your response to the roles being played around you. For example, some people become immediately tolerant and understanding when a friend discloses a personal problem. For them the role of "client" elicits the role of "therapist." So finding your own role behaviors in a particular situation is partially a matter of tuning into the role behaviors of the actors around you. (Conversely, exaggerating your own role behaviors in an exercise will help your partner define and play his or her role more sharply.)

If you want to help another actor play a king, bow to him.
LOUIS PALTER, 1970

Exercise 5–33: Role Games and the Text

1. Choose and memorize another dialogue from the appendix or use the one you memorized at the beginning of this chapter.

2. Play the dialogue using the same role games you chose for the last exercise. Repeat the dialogue three or four times. Begin by exaggerating your role; then gradually make it less outlandish and more realistic. Make the transition slowly.

3. Once again, complete the exercise by describing all the ways your partner expresses his or her chosen role.

Exercise 5–34: Role Enrichment

1. Repeat the last exercise three or four times. Use a different role game each time without changing the dialogue. It is important to have chosen your roles ahead of time so you do not have to pause and think each time you change roles.

2. Then, try "forgetting" the exercise and simply concentrate on one another. Trust the conditioning process. The effects of your work will cling without any special attention.

If you wish to know how your work is going, watch your fellow actors. If they are brilliant, it can only be because you are also.

ZBIGNEW CYNKUTIS, 1983

To commit yourself to ongoing, reciprocal communication with others is to allow these others to demand adjustment from you and for you to make the same demand of them. Much of what we are on stage depends on our ability to become "bewitched, bothered, and bewildered," turned on, put off, in-spired, and in-formed by others. Good acting is something that individual actors can often accomplish alone. But great acting is something that happens only *between* actors.

NOTES

1. I owe some of the steps in the last six exercises to Zbignew Cynkutis.

REFERENCES

Cohen, Robert. *Acting Power.* Mountain View, CA: Mayfield Publishing, 1978. The author's notion of "relacom," developed in Chapter 2, supplies some of the assumptions for my discussion of role games.

Dezseran, Louis John. *The Student Actor's Handbook*. Palo Alto, CA: Mayfield Publishing, 1975. See his chapter "Creating an Ensemble Approach with Other Actors."

Perls, F. S., Ralph Hefferline, and Paul Goodman. *Gestalt Therapy*. New York: Julian Press, 1951. A fairly technical introduction to gestalt principles, the book treats human relationships in a language that seems particularly applicable to acting.

Polster, Erving and Miriam. *Gestalt Therapy Integrated*. New York: Brunner/Mazel, 1973. The authors provide a particularly lucid and useful discussion of human contact and boundary making.

Stanislavski, Constantin. *An Actor Prepares*. New York: Theatre Arts Books, 1977 [thirtieth printing; first copyright, 1936]. See his chapter "Communion."

*(Notes, ideas,
sketches, reactions
to the exercises . . .)*

*(Notes, ideas,
sketches, reactions
to the exercises . . .)*

*(Notes, ideas,
sketches, reactions
to the exercises . . .)*

Working with the Environment

The interactions of dramatic characters always occur somewhere. In the theatre, that somewhere goes by a variety of names. The French, for example, refer to the where of a scene as the "*mise*" or the "*mise en scène.*" These terms are also used in the American theatre. But the more common labels are "setting," "environment," or just plain "space."

Settings can vary widely, from a watchpost on the parapet of Elsinore castle in *Hamlet* to the kitchen of the Loman family in *Death of a Salesman* to a subway car in *Dutchman*. Some settings are more fanciful than realistic. In plays like *Peer Gynt, Duck Hunting,* and *Waltz of the Toreadors,* settings may capture particular psychological states—say, a nightmare or fantasy.

Like the other given circumstances, the fictive environment, whether realistic or highly stylized, shapes how a character feels and behaves (i.e., lives) during each moment on stage. One of your major responsibilities is to ensure that the setting makes a difference to the character you are playing.

Imagine the same actor playing two roles in repertory, say, Biff in *Death of a Salesman* on Thursday and Clay in *Dutchman* on Saturday. Biff's first scene is in the familiar surroundings of his boyhood bedroom; Clay's, in a New York subway on a hot humid evening. It would be odd if the actor playing both characters responded to these settings in exactly the same way. The fictive environments are different, and each must play a distinctive role in influencing how the actor embodies these characters. On Thursdays and Saturdays, the actor changes more than just his lines, costumes, and makeup. Although he is working in the same theatre and on the same stage, he must be able to alter his sense of space according to the requirements of each environment.

Think of the hall, where you are hemmed in, or buoyed, or carried along, as the objects and the spaces change. Setting can astonish, or lull, or sing.

JOHN LAHR AND
JONATHAN PRICE,
LIFE SHOW

THE PARTICIPATORY PROCESS

In *The Reenchantment of the World,* Morris Berman offers a particularly useful word for talking about the ideal working relationship between actor and setting: *participation.* Berman explains it in ecological terms: (1) Participation is the kind of relationship that breaks down the customary separation between us and the environment. We and the nonhuman components in the space become connected and interdependent. (2) The environment is transformed from a mere group of objects to be acted upon into something with the capacity to act upon us in turn. (3) In a participatory relationship, we enter into a give-and-take with the environment that increases the variety, intensity, and depth of our reactions to it.

As a general rule, your aim on stage is to achieve and maintain as much participation with the setting as possible. This means you must allow the space to act upon you—that is, to shape your internal life as well as your physical movement. Instead of merely standing in, on, or in front of a setting, you must connect to it almost as though it were another actor always offering you something to respond to.

But participation is not easy. Human beings tend to reduce the charge they get from their habitats by becoming familiar with them. In everyday life, familiarity is sometimes useful because it helps people divorce themselves from surroundings that may be distracting or even somewhat painful. For example, right now I have managed to pretty much tune out the sound of traffic passing on the busy street near my home. Someone unfamiliar with the sound might find it extremely intrusive, at least for a short time. *The problem with familiarity is that it diminishes participation and dampens arousal—two deadly problems for an actor.*

Moreover, we often become familiar with a setting quickly, especially if it is one that reoccurs throughout the culture. Living rooms, kitchens, offices, bedrooms, depots, restaurants, street corners, bars, parlors, porches, and yards—all of which appear in many plays—have trouble eliciting and maintaining a participatory relationship. On stage, even settings that are not culturally typical tend to become eventually less evocative because of the frequency with which the actor is in them during rehearsal and performance. How then can an actor achieve Berman's version of participation with the environment?

An answer comes from a seemingly unlikely source: the American poet Walt Whitman. In his poem "I Saw in Louisiana a Live-Oak Growing," he creates a systematic method of participating in an environment that allows the environment to act upon the participant in a positive way. Although Whitman is not often associated with acting, what he has to say is nonetheless germane and relates directly to modern performance pedagogy (as I shall show later). His approach to participation has four interdependent parts (which will figure prominently in the exercises to come):

1. specific, detailed perception

2. association and memory

3. physical adjustment (motion)

4. heightened emotional response

The four parts of the participatory process are by no means entirely discrete. They are really phases that lead to and build on one another. Here is part of Whitman's scenario:

1. *Specific, detailed perception.* Although the poem is relatively short, the poet manages to recount several specific sensory details that provide the foundation for his involvement with the setting. He notes early on that the tree is a "live oak" that stands "all alone." Its leaves are "dark green." A detail of particular interest to Whitman is the "moss [that hangs] down from the branches." Later in the poem, after going through other parts of his process, he notices that the tree "glistens in a wide flat space."

2. *Association and memory.* The personal associations and memories evoked by the perceptual details are rich. Most important is that the tree reminds Whitman of his own body. ("And its look . . . made me think of myself.") Because it stands "alone," the tree also "makes [him] think of" human companionship and intimacy.

3. *Physical adjustments.* The poet's movement is simple and very specific. He approaches the tree, reaches up, and breaks "off a twig with a certain number of leaves." Next, he places the twig "in sight in [his] room."

4. *Heightened emotional response.* The intensification of the poet's emotional life becomes clear in his diction. He experiences the tree's leaves as "joyous," a word he uses at three different points in the poem. Some of his feelings about the tree's looks are the same as those he has about his own body: He and the tree look "rude, unbending, and lusty." But perhaps the most complex and poignant of the poet's feelings surround his conviction about the difference between the tree and himself: While the oak can stand "solitary" and still be "joyous," the poet cannot. Unlike the tree, he is unable to live "without a friend . . . near."

This outline of Whitman's involvement with his setting is significant only because it helps to clarify the different parts of the process at work. *More important is the way the four stages of participation occur and reoccur in varying sequences, always heightening and augmenting one another.* If we were to diagram the process, it would be circular rather than linear, always revolving back upon itself and becoming more powerful as it does so. In Whitman's poem, perception leads to feelings that stimulate associations and memories. These trigger more feelings that give rise to first one physical adjustment, then another. The motion elicits more associations and memories, followed by still more detailed perceptions that evoke feelings heightened to the level of conviction.[1]

Besides the fact that he has given us a practical outline for working with the stage environment, there is yet another reason for lingering over Whitman in this chapter. His particular version of the participatory process sheds light on the methods of two very influential acting teachers, Lee Strasberg and Jerzy Grotowski.

Both approach the stage environment using some of the features found in Whitman's system. But each emphasizes certain parts of the poet's process while deemphasizing others. For example, Grotowski stresses specific kinds of physical movement as a means of altering the actor's usual perceptual patterns and arousing associations, memories, and feelings. Strasberg, on the other hand, links specific perceptual details from the setting with personal sense memories from the actor's past in order to evoke a full inner life.

Whitman helps us recognize that both Strasberg and Grotowski really focus on selected portions of a much broader and more holistic method of working with space. The next four groups of exercises try to give equal time and emphasis to each step in Whitman's approach to participation. (I hope one of the by-products of these exercises will be to restore the practices of Strasberg and Grotowski to the larger context, provided by Whitman, where they seem to belong and which makes them appear complementary rather than disparate.)

EXERCISES

The purpose of the exercises is to help you learn to use the four phases of Whitman's process in a way that will enable you to personalize your spatial surroundings on stage. Because the phases are supposed to "intertwingle," each of the following sequences begins with a different part of the process but then moves on to include the others.

Beginning with Perceptual Details

How you respond to the environment around you is influenced by your perceptual habits, by the normal ways you sense and take in your setting. One of the outcomes of your usual perceptual style is the tendency to focus automatically on certain physical details in a space, while letting others slip by. The details you select are tied closely to your usual style of orientation and coordination. Orientation lets you tell up from down, left from right. Coordination is what enables you to put movements together into purposeful sequences. Both work together with sense perception to help determine how you behave in response to a setting. For example, depending on habit, some of you might enter your apartments by looking at the doorknob, putting your hand on it, then stepping up and forward onto the threshold, without glancing down at your feet. Others may proceed in the opposite way: first, looking down and stepping up, then reaching for the doorknob. One way to begin expanding and intensifying the way you react to various settings is by learning to vary the perceptual details you focus on to cue your physical organization.

Exercise 6–1: Eye Rotation and Visual Selection

1. With a partner choose and memorize a short dialogue. What kind of environment does the text seem to suggest? Arrange a simple setting in the acting space: maybe just a table and chairs, or a platform with square blocks to sit on. The set, however makeshift, is your character's physical world. By using this and the other exercises in the chapter, you will learn to allow that world to give your responses a particular shape. That shape is part of the character. (I say "part of" because many other influences help to shape a character, such as the rest of the given circumstances, actions, stakes, and so on.)

2. Lie on your back in the center of the space and slowly spread your arms and legs until you've formed a large X.

3. Gradually roll your eyes in a 360° circle, first clockwise, then counterclockwise. In this step you are relying more than usual on your peripheral vision to see various bits and pieces of your setting.

4. Roll your eyes one more time. After you complete this rotation, choose some specific element that stood out for you (e.g., the corner of a platform, a button on a chair, a dust ball on the floor—the more specific the better).

5. Go and examine the element closely. As you do so, allow a specific association or image to arise. It might be something fanciful or something from the past.

6. Repeat the exercise three to five times from different spots in the acting space. Locate a new visual detail with each repetition and focus on the associations and images that arise from examining it.

Guidelines: Both the angle of vision and the use of your eyes are unusual. The idea is to see and experience your setting differently, from the lowest plane your eyes are capable of instead of from the highest (which is the normal vantage point). There are no ideal or correct targets for your perception. Whatever piece of the setting interests you or gets your attention is the right object of focus.

Exercise 6–2: Sound, Hearing, and the Perception of Space

1. Sit in the middle of the same acting area.

2. (a) Bounce a sharp vowel off the ceiling so it comes right back at you. (b) Fill the entire space with the sound of a short phrase or single word from the text you have memorized. (c) Now, use your voice to "hit" each of the three to five visual targets you discovered in the preceding exercise. (Think of the sound as making a straight line from your mouth to a button on a chair, a crack in a bench, a smudge on the wall, or whatever.)

3. Listen carefully to what the setting does to the sound, both as you vocalize it and just after. (What you don't hear is as important as what you do. In some cases you may hear an echo; in others not. Sometimes you might hear a faint ringing sound as you speak. At other times, the sound may seem muffled or somehow lacking in volume.)

4. Try to get a specific image or association for each sound impression you receive while doing step 3. For example, if you hear an echo, you might get an image of a huge cave or a canyon. If your voice rings off the surfaces of the setting, you might associate the sound with sleigh bells or the high-pitched yelps of a lonely puppy.

Guidelines: The images and associations you receive are part of your reaction to the setting—reactions made available by listening carefully to what the environment does to your voice. Images and associations may be only the beginning of a whole series of responses. Be aware of emotional states and impulses to move, or behave in certain specific ways.

It is sometimes easier to think of a setting simply in terms of what we see rather than what we hear. The sound exercise brings the setting in on another perceptual channel (hearing), which can augment the amount of physical and psychological stimulation it offers us.

Exercise 6–3: Environmental Texture: Warm/Cold

1. With a partner, take off your shoes and socks and walk about the setting. While one of you finds the warmest spot, the other should look for the coldest.

2. Once you have found your places, find movement that brings as much of the physical surface into contact with your body as possible. For example, rub your cheek against it, then your forehead, the backs of your arms, and the small of your back.

3. Work slowly and pay particular attention to whatever images, feelings, or impulses might occur.

4. Let go of your work and do your dialogue three or four times, focusing on one another.

Exercise 6–4: Environmental Texture: Rough/Smooth

1. Repeat the exercise. This time one of you find the roughest surface on the setting; the other, the smoothest.

Exercise 6–5: Environmental Texture: Soft/Hard

1. Do the exercise again. One of you find the softest surface; the other, the hardest.

Beginning with Associations and Memories

In the last chapter, I noted that the people we are with in the present often remind us of people from the past. Something similar can happen with settings. The one we are in can evoke memories of places from the past. These associations from former environments can allow the present setting to trigger a richer and more compelling array of feelings and impulses than it might otherwise provoke.

By choosing carefully which associations and memories you actually work with in the following exercises, you can influence the sort of emotional impact your setting has on you and the types of movement it is likely to inspire.

Places become reservoirs of significant life experiences lying at the center of a person's identity and sense of psychological well-being.

MICHAEL A. GODKIN, FROM *THE HUMAN EXPERIENCE OF SPACE AND PLACE*

Exercise 6–6: Transformations

1. Set up the acting space to fit the dialogue. You may use the setting from the previous exercises or choose another.

2. Spend two or three minutes repeating your dialogue to one another while you move around exploring the setting. Make sure you touch all the elements you have placed in the space.

3. As you explore, become aware of what other settings come to mind through memory or association. For example, a simple kitchen setting may remind you of a baseball diamond, a tennis court, or a courtroom.

4. Consult with your partner and choose three or four associations that interest both of you, or, in some way, seem to "fit" the text you have memorized. Go with your first impressions.

5. Rearrange the space into each of the settings you have chosen.

6. "Live" in each new setting for two to five minutes by improvising an activity that fits. For instance, if a kitchen has been transformed into a battlefield, improvise a battle by using the table and chairs as cover and throwing wadded up napkins and styrofoam cups at one another. Incorporate the lines from your dialogue, allowing your physical activity to dictate the tone of your verbal exchange.

Exercise 6–7: Back to Home Base

1. After experimenting with several transformations, rearrange the environment into the setting you began with.

2. "Forget" the exercises and see what happens when you go back to simply concentrating on each other.

Transforming the original setting—be it a plain outside Thebes or a kitchen—according to pertinent memories and associations is a way of assigning a variety of specific roles to the original environment. When you transform a kitchen into a courtroom, you are giving yourself the opportunity to experience the kitchen anew *in the role of a courtroom*. The original setting is neither forgotten nor left behind (especially since eventually you must come back to it), but it has been given the capacity to evoke a broader repertory of reactions.

Beginning with Movement

A major theme in this book is that the muscular behavior of the body is part of your perceptual, mental, and emotional activity. Seen in this light, a setting, because it guides your physical motion and alignment, also has a profound influence on your inner life.

The following exercises work from the outside in, using physical movement that triggers inward responses.

Exercise 6–8: Exploring a Setting with Movement

1. Select one to three components of your setting. These may range from the arm of a chair or a spot on the floor to the edge of a step unit or the seam where two platforms join. Be specific.

2. Explore each detail by moving in relation to it. Discover how many ways you can blend or join your body to the element you have chosen. For example, if you are working with a step, you might lie on it, spread your arms along its width, kneel on it.

3. It is important that you move more or less continuously from one position to the next. Try to develop a simple ease and fluidity.

4. As you move, first pay attention to your bodily sensations. After a minute or two, begin to focus on whatever images, associations, memories, or feelings arise. Let these determine the dynamics of your movement (i.e., speed, size, direction, and overall flow).

5. Work for three to seven minutes with each of the spatial details you have chosen.

Guidelines: Remember you are exploring the setting with your body. You are under no obligation to entertain anyone or create some sort of mime show.

Exercise 6–9: Incorporating the Voice

1. Repeat the exercise, allowing your movement to pull sounds out of you.

Exercise 6–10: Incorporating Your Partner

1. Working with a partner, construct a simple setting for your dialogue.

2. Begin adjusting and blending with the structures you have chosen (as in the previous exercises). Work independently at first.

3. Make sure to take some time to focus on the interior life the movement helps instigate. After a minute or two, start exchanging lines from your memorized text *while you continue your physical work.*

Guidelines: There is no need to worry about one another's exact location (as long as you do not interfere with one another). But you do have to listen carefully while you are moving.

Exercise 6–11: Back to the Text

1. Sit or stand on or near the part of the setting you were working with.

2. Concentrate on your partner and play your dialogue.

Guidelines: The more you can let go of the exercises and focus on your partner, the greater impact the exercises will have.

Beginning with Feelings

Sometimes stage settings evoke feelings spontaneously, without requiring a lot of preliminary work. This occurs offstage too. For example, visitors to medieval Gothic cathedrals often feel immediately overwhelmed by the mystery and majesty that surrounds them. Natural settings can have a similar impact. The way the sky holds the light during late winter in the northern Midwest can bring instant delight, even with snow piled high all around.

The more work you do with openness and stillness, the more likely it is that a stage setting will trigger a definite mood unsolicited. When a specific feeling takes hold, there is a lot you can do with it. The following exercises will help you use your spontaneous feelings to lead you on to memories and associations, specific movement patterns, and to new ways of seeing and sensing (perceiving) your setting. As in Whitman's poem, all of these effects react back upon your initial feelings, allowing them to become deeper, more sensitive to the space, more specific, and at the same time more varied through time.

Exercise 6–12: Environmental History

1. Join your partner in arranging a simple setting for the dialogue you have memorized.

2. Without consulting one another, each of you find a separate element (chair, table, shadow, angle of a platform) that evokes a specific mood. Take your time; it is very important that you do not force yourself to have feelings. You may want to relax by taking a deep breath and "letting go" of tension as you exhale. Any mood will do. It need not be terribly intense to begin with, just noticeable to you.

3. Now, as you have done in some of the previous exercises, let the spatial element you have chosen remind you of something from your past. (Notice here that the feeling connected to the element you have selected will guide your memory.)

4. To intensify the impact of your memories, take turns relating them out loud. Keep the account brief. For example, "This table reminds me of the one we had at home when I was ten or eleven. [Breathe fully.] On Thanksgiving, Christmas, and birthdays, we would gather around it. Each of us had our own place. I sat there. [Remember to keep breathing fully.] My sister over there. Mom at that end and dad at the other." That's all you need—something short and easy to share with others.

5. Now, move in the space in a way consistent with the short history you have just narrated. If the table is the source of your short story, you might go through the motions of setting it for a family feast; then sit down and pass a plate for your father to fill; next blow out the candles on an imagined birthday cake. The various activities need not be closely related, nor do they have to all come from a single remembered occasion. Just follow your memories from one set of movements to another.

Guidelines: There is no need to plan each movement ahead of time. Just let them come. Move continuously and fluidly without stopping or hurrying. Follow your energy impulses. Exaggerate the movement sometimes; at other times move more conventionally.

Exercise 6–13: Connecting the Text

1. Do this exercise with a partner. The purpose of the exercise is to allow the impact of the previous exercise to influence your dialogue work.

2. Position yourselves on or near the part of the setting you each were working with in the previous exercise.

3. Once again wait for a specific feeling to form. It doesn't matter whether it is the same or different from the feeling you started with in the last exercise.

4. Repeat your memorized dialogue three or four times. Concentrate on one another. Let the residues from the previous exercise cling to the short dialogue.

The last two exercises employ two different kinds of subtext: one verbal (the story of a particular setting from your past), the other physical (the movements that go with the setting). The written play is the point of intersection, where both subtexts join and hopefully become part of you as you are doing the exercise.

Costumes and Properties

Costumes and props are spatial objects that move with the actor. A number of clichés run through much of the pedagogy dealing with the use of props and costumes. Most of these have a tone of stern warning: "Use the prop, but don't let the prop use you"; "The worse the actor, the more noticeable the costume." All of these are exaggerations, but they do indicate something important. Costumes and properties do not exist for their own sake but fulfill a double function: First, as part of the environmental circumstances, they help to evoke responses in an actor; and, second, as extensions of the actor's body, they are a means of communicating with others on stage. In performance, the two functions become one since an actor's responses are always supposed to be fundamentally communicative.

The approach to properties and costumes is similar to the approach to settings. Once again, detailed sense perception, memory and association, kinesthetic investment, and heightened feelings form the basis for the upcoming work. The next several exercises will help you become more responsive to costumes and props and expand the various ways you use them to communicate with others.

Exercise 6–14: Guessing Game

1. Work with a partner.

2. Choose a prop or costume and focus on some visual detail. The more particular the better. For example, focusing on a piece of thread hanging from a pocket is better than just noticing the pocket.

3. Wear or manipulate the object in a way that emphasizes the detail you notice so that your partner can guess what it is. Vary your activities until he or she is successful.

4. Be aware of whatever associations, memories, feeling, or impulses arise as you work with the item.

5. Then switch roles with your partner.

6. Continue taking turns for three or four minutes, or until you run out of specific visual details that you can communicate by wearing or manipulating the item in some way.

Guidelines: In order to give your inner life some emphasis, you may want to pause after the exercise and mention some of what you experienced.

Exercise 6–15: Including Your Text

1. Begin by repeating the last exercise, but this time use a different item.

2. As you go through the exercise, speak to one another using the lines from the dialogue you have memorized for this chapter.

3. To simplify your work, you need to eliminate the guessing game you used in the last exercise. Keep the dialogue continuous while you (a) discover a visual detail, (b) wear or use the item in a way that shows off the detail, and (c) pass the item to your partner.

Guidelines: Don't worry about how your lines sound. Let your work with the costume or prop determine the tone and rhythm of your dialogue.

Exercise 6–16: Hot and Cold

1. Select an ordinary prop or costume piece.

2. Imagine the item is very hot and wear or use it accordingly.

3. Then imagine it is ice cold.

4. Stay tuned to your inner life. Hot and cold are provocative sense impressions.

5. Give your partner a turn.

Exercise 6–17: Application to the Text

1. Complete the last exercise again while saying your dialogue.

Exercise 6–18: Moving with the Help of . . .

1. Select a simple property (fork, spoon, glass, book, and so on).
2. Explore how many different ways you can use the prop to help you move. Walk, run, jump, crawl, roll, dance—move in as many ways as possible.
3. Use the prop so that it actually facilitates your movement.
4. Let the size and speed of your movement vary according to the tone and intensity of whatever inner life your movement stimulates.

Guidelines: One way to use a prop as a facilitator is to find ways it can make your movement more enjoyable.

Exercise 6–19: Movement, Text, and Partner

1. Have your partner join you in the acting space.
2. Each of you should have a different prop.
3. Move about the space randomly with the help of your props.
4. As you do so, exchange lines.
5. Continue for three or four minutes. The movement need not "make sense." The more varied the better.

Guidelines: As usual, there is no need to work for a full performance. Just allow the work you've done in the first part of the exercise to creep into your work in step 5 without any special effort. Chances are good that you will have assimilated the prop into your expressive behavior. If not, repeat the last two exercises. There's no hurry. Learning that stays with us often takes time.

Exercise 6–20: Costume Invention

1. Select a simple costume piece and invent as many different ways of wearing it as you can. A pair of shoes might become gloves, ear muffs, shoulder pads. A jacket can serve as a cape, an umbrella, a skirt.
2. Your aim is to move continuously but without hurry from one way of using your costume to another.
3. Be aware of the various psychological and emotional states that occur during your work.

Exercise 6–21: Text and Partner

1. Do the same exercise with a partner.

2. As you both change ways of wearing your costume pieces, exchange lines from your dialogue.

3. Take two to five minutes to gradually arrive at one way of wearing your costume.

4. Then concentrate on one another without worrying about your costumes. Repeat the text for two to three minutes.

Guidelines: As with the prop exercises, the goal is to integrate your costume into your responsive communication with the other actor. Again, results must come "by the way." The focus in step 4 should be on your partner only.

Exercise 6–22: Cross-Dressing

1. Select a simple costume piece.

2. Put it on your partner and arrange it.

3. As you do so, exchange lines from your dialogue.

4. When you have finished, let your partner return the favor.

Exercise 6–23: Dancing with Your Costume

1. Bring to class a recording of dance music from the Big Band Era. Select a piece that you feel captures the mood of the jump or scene you have memorized.

2. Dance with your costume as though it were another person. Exaggerate your movements. The more outlandish the better.

Exercise 6–24: Dancing in Your Costume

1. Put on the costume piece and dance with your partner, who should also be wearing his or her costume.

2. The dance should be improvised and need not have prearranged steps. You do not have to touch each other, or even be close.

3. As you dance, exchange lines from your dialogue.

Guidelines: The dancing can take any form you wish, as long as you accept the discipline (mood, rhythm, and tempo) of the music you have chosen.

Exercise 6–25: Fading Out of the Dance

1. Begin the previous exercise again.

2. Join the dialogue to your work. That is, talk while you dance.

3. After two or three passes through your dialogue, have someone fade the music out slowly. As the volume decreases, make the dance movement smaller. Your dancing should disappear at the same time the music fades out.

4. Repeat your dialogue two or three more times without dancing.

Guidelines: Trust your work and have fun.

Exercise 6–26: From Association and Memory to Movement

1. Select a prop or costume piece that goes with your dialogue.

2. Inspect it carefully.

3. As you do so, allow it to remind you of a similar item from your past.

4. Give a brief account of your memory. For example, "This pencil reminds me of the one my first-grade teacher gave me. I remember copying the letters of my name. It was the first time I realized what a long name I had."

5. Now use (i.e., move) the item in a way consistent with your story. (Take a piece of paper and print your name slowly in big letters, the way a child might. Then write the numbers from one to ten; next you might print the alphabet or some simple words.)

6. Give your partner the opportunity to do the exercise.

Guidelines: If you use a costume piece, you may find yourself putting it on and wearing it in different ways depending on what clothing from your past it reminds you of. For instance, a pair of pants might remind you of the jeans you wore on your first campout and/or of the long, floppy rabbit ears that went with your Halloween costume when you were nine.

Exercise 6–27: Moving Toward the Text

1. Now, wear, hold, or use the costume or prop in a way that fits your text.

2. Play the dialogue in the acting space with your partner.

3. Concentrate on one another and allow the item you have chosen to become part of your responses and communication.

Guidelines: If you do not feel the prop or costume is helping you to respond and communicate sufficiently, repeat the exercise again. This time work more slowly.

To live fully is to live resonantly.

T. ROSZAK, *WHERE THE WASTELAND ENDS*

Imagine a small, delicate tuning fork made of stainless steel. With the fork comes a miniature mallet. Strike the fork gently with the mallet and you get a pure, shimmering tone that seems somehow larger than the force that produced it. This image is important because it summarizes the ideal relationship between the actor and his or her spatial surroundings (and perhaps the rest of the given circumstances as well). The actor's job is to resonate as fully as possible to whatever impulses the environment has to offer.

The image cannot quite tell the whole truth, however. For, it is the actor who *transforms* the setting into a field of potent external impulses. This capacity does not come automatically. An actor must learn a process that brings the setting to life. In so doing, she learns to bring herself to life.

NOTES

1. A version of participation similar to Whitman's may be found in the work of other Romantics as well, such as Blake, Thoreau, and Emerson.

REFERENCES

Berman, Morris. *The Reenchantment of the World.* Ithaca, NY: Cornell University Press, 1981. Berman's book is a critique of nineteenth- and twentieth-century empiricism. Part of his point is that classical science provides just one way of knowing the world, a way that has both advantages and disadvantages. Perhaps its biggest disadvantage is the sense of separation between the individual and whatever he or she is studying. *Participation* is the term Berman uses for an approach to knowing that acknowledges the connection between self and the rest of the world.

Buttimer, Anne, and David Seamon, eds. *The Human Experience of Space and Place.* London: Croom Helm, 1980. The editors offer a variety of essays about the different ways people experience their environments. While the language is technical, taken from phenomenology, the insights are worth the work.

Hull, Loraine S. *Strasberg's Method as Taught by Lorrie Hull: A Practical Guide for Actors, Teachers, and Directors.* Woodbridge, CT: Ox Box Publishers, 1985. The author describes the basic exercises that make up the main body of Strasberg's pedagogy. Her authority comes from a long association with the Actor's Studio, both as a student and teacher.

Lahr, John, and Jonathan Price. *Life Show.* New York: Viking Press, 1973.

Mehrabian, Albert. *Public Places and Private Spaces: The Psychology of Work, Play, and Living Environments.* New York: Basic Books, 1976. The book is a lively introduction to the field of ecological psychology, written for a broad audience.

Miller, Edwin Haviland. *Whitman "Leaves of Grass": Selections.* New York: Appleton-Century-Crofts, 1970. The poem about the oak tree is on page 112.

Morphos, Evangeline, ed. *A Dream of Passion.* New York: New American Library, 1987. Assembled from Strasberg's unpublished writing, the book explains the Method.

Roszak, Theodore. *Where the Wasteland Ends: Politics and Transcendence in Postindustrial Society.* Garden City, NY: Doubleday, 1972.

Wicker, Allan W. *An Introduction to Ecological Psychology.* Belmont, CA: Wadsworth, 1979. More technical than Mehrabian's, Wicker's book introduces the standard questions and research techniques in the field of ecological psychology.

(Notes, ideas,
sketches, reactions
to the exercises . . .)

_____

_____

_____

_____

_____

_____

_____

_____

_____

_____

_____

_____

_____

_____

_____

_____

_____

_____

_____

_____

_____

_____

*(Notes, ideas,
sketches, reactions
to the exercises . . .)*

ACTOR'S JOURNAL

*(Notes, ideas,
sketches, reactions
to the exercises . . .)*

_____

_____

_____

_____

_____

_____

_____

_____

_____

_____

_____

_____

_____

_____

_____

_____

_____

_____

_____

Working with Events

An event is whatever is happening to you at a particular moment. You pull up to a stop sign and begin to ease into the intersection when suddenly you hear the squeal of breaks as another car bangs into your rear bumper. This is happening to you; that is, *you are the receiver of energy* that has the potential to change you in some way: hurt you, scare you, annoy you, startle you. *Events are energy systems that impinge upon you at a particular moment.* Not all are as exciting as a car wreck. At any one given time, you are being pleased, conned, bossed around, seduced, fed, bothered. What makes these events is that you *are not doing but getting done to.* The energy is incoming.

The actor's job is to make himself or herself responsive to events on stage. All too often, however, it is easy to get caught up in a game of evasion in order to escape from whatever event is going on in the here and now. The purpose of this chapter is to help you both recognize the events happening to your character and respond to them deeply and honestly.

Event: n. 1. anything that happens or is regarded as happening; an occurrence, esp. one of some importance. . . . 3. something that occurs in a certain place during a particular interval of time.

THE RANDOM HOUSE DICTIONARY OF THE ENGLISH LANGUAGE

TWO GAMES OF EVASION: THE PAST AND THE FUTURE

Modern rationalist psychology features past events as the basic building blocks of individual identity. The fact that I can remember a sequence of events extending back through time, all of which happened to the same "me" assures me that I am who I think I am. I'm the one Steven Lampke threw into a brick wall on the second day of kindergarten; the person Sister Mary Daniel got on for forgetting homework; the one who played second base in Little League; and so forth. The fact that I can identify all of these events as having happened to me in the past gives me my sense of a more or less continuous, single identity.

For many of us, answering the question, "What happened to you yesterday?" is much easier than answering the question, "What is happening to you right now?" The personal stories that portray our continuity always stop just before the present begins. A present event is elusive largely because it is still incomplete, still unfolding, still forming, and therefore still unformed. As such, it may threaten to destabilize whatever secure sense of identity we get from a past that feels more complete than the now.

The present is elusive for yet another reason. Recognizing and focusing on the event we are actually living often distracts from what is sometimes the primary business of life: getting to the next moment. In American culture, the future is frequently more important than the present. A common habit is to justify the present in terms of the future: "I am doing X now, so I can get Y tomorrow." This grammatical form is more than the basis for an idiom; it is a strategy for living that is all too easy for us to bring on stage.

In performance, looking ahead is especially hard to avoid because you have read the script and attended rehearsals; so you know with some precision where everything is leading. In an effort to do a good job, you might feel tempted to prepare yourself for an upcoming event before you have finished experiencing the one you are in. For example, maybe you start thinking about your next line instead of listening to what your partner is saying to you. Or, you might start planning that difficult downstage cross when you are really supposed to be enjoying a wonderfully dry martini.

Some acting teachers call getting ahead of yourself "anticipation." Anticipating what comes next is a product of insecurity, a reaction to the need to feel in control of the future. But in performance, anticipating produces an important irony. Getting ahead actually undermines your future on stage. Engaging the present event as fully as possible is the true foundation of your next moment—the stimulus for going on with your ongoing life on stage. You must allow the present to nourish you in order to make a vibrant future possible.

To be sure, past and future are important to the work of actors, but not as games of evasion. I will discuss their importance in Chapter 11 on motivation.

Each moment on stage contributes to an event that is coming to be. But in the theatre an event is invisible to an audience, unless someone on stage experiences it. Usually that someone is an actor who is playing a character. The more deeply and thoroughly you experience an event on stage as an actor, the clearer and more concrete it can be for an audience.

EXERCISES

Focusing on Events

One way to begin experiencing the event that is unfolding in a particular moment is by using the following paradigm:

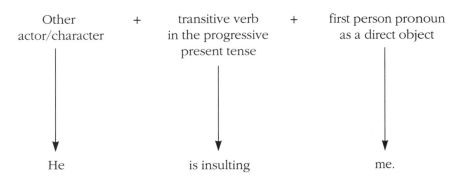

Other actor/character + transitive verb in the progressive present tense + first person pronoun as a direct object

He   is insulting   me.

The *other* actor/character is the subject of the sentence. A transitive verb in the present progressive tense (*-ing*) captures what he or she *is doing* to you. The direct object, "me," stands for you and the character you are playing. This formulation might come from Ophelia in III.1, when Hamlet tells her to go to a nunnery. The precise formulation would be "Hamlet is insulting me." But there are many ways to interpret Ophelia (and the word *nunnery*), so several other formulations are also possible: "Hamlet is teasing me"; "Hamlet is embarrassing me" (after all, the king, the queen, and the girl's father are all listening to her conversation with the prince).

For a variation of the same paradigm, use "making me feel" as the progressive verb and follow it with an adverb or an adjective (colloquial grammar is OK): "Hamlet is making me feel nervous."

The formulation you choose should not center on what you think Hamlet actually intends to do to Ophelia but on how you/she actually takes in what is happening. In other words, always formulate an event from the subjective position of the character you are playing.

Even if your character has no lines, there is usually still plenty happening to you. For example, on at least two occasions, Laura (in *The Glass Menagerie*) is silent while her brother and mother quarrel. To make contact with the event, you might try: "My mother and brother are making me feel nauseous"; or, more simply: "This fight is making me sick."

Exercise 7–1: Verbalizing the Event I

1. Choose one character in the following excerpt.
2. Try to verbalize what is happening to you-as-the-character. Make sure to use the paradigm given above.

From *Winners* by Brian Friel:

MAG: You never proposed to me.

JOE: What?

MAG: You haven't *asked* me to marry you.

JOE: What are you raving about?

MAG: Propose to me.

JOE: God!

MAG: Now.

JOE: You really are . . .

MAG: Ask me.

Guidelines: Avoid merely paraphrasing the text. Paraphrasing is particularly easy in the case of Joe, whose version of the event might be: "She is making me propose." No fair, though, because you are merely summarizing Mag's words to you. Try to make the verb as physical as possible. Verbs that help the event get into your body are best.

Exercise 7–2: Verbalizing the Event II

1. Do the same exercise again, but with the following excerpt. This time try to find two or three alternate formulations of the event, based on differing interpretations.

From *Sexual Perversity in Chicago* by David Mamet:

Dan and Deb in bed in his apartment.

DANNY: Well.

DEBORAH: Well.

DANNY: Yeah, well, hey . . . uh . . . (*Pause.*) I feel *great.* (*Pause.*) You?

DEBORAH: Uh huh.

DANNY: Yup. (*Pause.*) You, uh you have to go to work (you work, right?) you have to go to work tomorrow?

DEBORAH: Yes. Well . . .

DANNY: You're going home?

DEBORAH: Do you want me to?

DANNY: Only if you want to. Do you want to?

DEBORAH: Do you want me to stay? I don't know if it's such a good idea that I stay here tonight.

DANNY: Why? (*Pause.*) I'd like you to stay. If you'd like to.

Guidelines: For the sake of simplicity, read this unit as possessing just one event for each actor.

Giving Events Specific Impact

Because events in the present are so slippery, using the verbal paradigm given earlier is an important first step in recognizing and connecting to what is happening to you. But putting the event into words is only a beginning. The next few exercises will give you ways of helping events have a specific impact on you.

Exercise 7–3: Color Imagination

1. Memorize a new scene or jump. If you wish, use one of the excerpts included in the last two exercises.
2. Use the verbal paradigm to determine what is happening to you.
3. Next, decide whether what is happening to you is positive or negative.
4. Depending on your choice in step 3, imagine swallowing and inhaling your favorite (positive) or least favorite (negative) color. Taste it on your tongue. Feel it going down your throat when you swallow, then into your stomach and intestines. Now, inhale the color into your lungs and feel it fill your heart.
5. Imagine you have actually turned that color.
6. By blowing, exhale the color all over the set, props, and the actor you are working with.

Exercise 7–4: Incorporating Your Voice

1. Repeat the last exercise.
2. If you are working with a positive color, exhale on the syllables "ha ha" or "ho ho." If the color is negative, exhale on "no" or "oh no."

Exercise 7–5: Adding the Text

1. Join your partner in the acting space.
2. Repeat the last exercise.
3. But exhale on one key word from the text you have memorized.
4. Alternate so that the exercise works as a dialogue.
5. Repeat the exercise for three or four minutes. Every so often choose a different word to exhale on. Remember to choose only words you believe are particularly important.

Guidelines: Regardless of what word(s) you have chosen, make sure to keep the same explosive quality as you achieved with "ho ho" or "oh no."

Exercise 7–6: Including the Rest of the Text

1. Now let go of the exercise and simply talk to one another using the dialogue you have memorized.

2. Trust the exercise to transfer to your work without your having to think about it.

Exercise 7–7: Sound Improvisation

1. Once again, define what is happening to you by making yourself the object of a transitive verb. Maybe your definition of the event has changed in light of the last few exercises.

2. Find a specific sound that summarizes your reaction to what is happening to you. It may be a scream, groan, or a happy laugh. Avoid using an actual word.

3. Repeat the sound several times, exaggerating it as much as possible. Concentrate on the sensations the sound creates in your body.

Exercise 7–8: Sound and Motion Improvisation

1. Repeat the last exercise.

2. Find a movement that matches the sound. For example, you might recoil in horror as you scream, or you might double over as you groan, or jump up and down in time with your laughter. The bigger the movement the better.

3. Make sure to repeat the sound and movement combination several times, three to five minutes.

4. Pay attention to associations, feelings, impulses—the inner dimension of your experience.

Exercise 7–9: Sound and Motion Improvisation with a Partner

1. Form a dialogue by exchanging sound and motion with a partner. Allow the dialogue to become free and spontaneous. Use as much of the acting space as possible.

2. Gradually, substitute a key word from your script for the sounds you are making.

3. Change the word you are using three or four times.

Guidelines: Let the exercise last awhile (four to six minutes). Maintain the vocal quality of your original utterance (i.e., your scream, laugh, groan, or whatever). Also, keep your movement exaggerated.

Exercise 7–10: Back to the Text

1. Take a moment to relax. The last two exercises required a lot of movement.

2. Now do the dialogue "straight" without worrying about transferring the exercises you've done. Repeat it three or four times or until you can concentrate on your partner without distraction.

Exercise 7–11: Metaphoric Exploration

1. Begin by reviewing the definition of what is happening to you in the dialogue you are using.

2. Find a metaphor or simile that describes the character's overall sense of the event. For example, "He/she is manipulating me" = "I feel like a wind-up toy." "He/she is killing me" = "I feel like a bug being crushed."

3. Now, explore the metaphor using all the sounds and movements it suggests.

4. Enacting a wind-up toy or a bug about to be crushed helps you develop a full psychophysical sense of the event. This feeling-connection to what is happening to you will trigger a very definite reaction—an impulse to resist, embrace, escape, and so on whatever the event is.

5. Allow your partner to do the exercise.

Guidelines: To focus your attention on discovering a useful metaphor, start with the phrase "I feel like a . . . " (The word *feel* does not refer only to emotions but also to the entire experience the event creates in you, including its muscular sensations.)

Exercise 7–12: Metaphor as Dialogue

1. Continue the previous exercise with a partner.

2. Each of you pick a metaphor. Then enact a dialogue of sounds and movements based upon the metaphors you have chosen. For example, one of you might make the sounds and movements of a wind-up toy; the other might respond with those of a bug being crushed.

Exercise 7–13: Coming Back to the Text

1. Repeat the last exercise again.

2. Allow about one minute; then start to use the words of your jump or scene.

3. Gradually go back to normal movement and postures and to your own natural way of speaking. Use from three to seven minutes.

4. Once you have returned to a more realistic mode of expression, continue the dialogue for another minute, concentrating as much as possible on the other actor rather than on the exercise you have just completed.

Connecting Events with Others

The way you experience an event in a particular moment on stage is partially in the hands of your fellow actors, who are doing something to you (whether directly or indirectly). The next few exercises will help you develop responses to an event that are specific to the particular actor you are working with. The work you did in Chapter 5 is a good preparation for these exercises.

Exercise 7–14: Associating the Event with the Other Actor

1. Join your partner in the acting space and make eye contact in silence for about thirty seconds before going on.

2. Formulate the event that is happening to you in the dialogue. But this time focus on your partner by using the pronoun "you" in place of the other character's name. For example, instead of "Mag is badgering me," use "you are badgering me" (Joe from *Winners*). Instead of "Danny is seducing me," try "You are seducing me" (Deborah from *Sexual Perversity*).

3. Then add the phrase "aren't you?" to the end of the line—for example, "You are badgering me, aren't you?" or "You're seducing me, aren't you?"

4. Repeat the simple questions ending in "aren't you" several times as a dialogue with your partner.

5. At the same time, move randomly around the acting space but do not touch. (Make sure to maintain eye contact.)

Exercise 7–15: Back to the Text

1. Go back to your original dialogue.

2. Concentrate on one another. Move or don't move—whichever feels most natural.

3. Repeat the dialogue several times, until you feel that you're really talking to one another without worrying about whether the previous exercise has had an effect on your work.

Exercise 7–16: "Stop"/"Keep On"

1. Go back to exercise 7–14.

2. Replace "you" with "stop" or "keep on," depending on whether your character likes or dislikes the event that is happening. Also remove the phrase "aren't you?"—for example, "*Stop* badgering me" (Joe in *Winners*) or "*Keep on* seducing me" (Deborah in *Sexual Perversity*).

3. Now, do a dialogue with your partner based on this new formulation of the event.

4. Make sure to maintain eye contact and to move on impulse.

Exercise 7–17: Back to the Text

1. Maintain the eye contact and the movement.

2. But use your original script.

3. Repeat the dialogue until you can concentrate on one another without monitoring your work.

The actor's task is to translate the character from a creature predetermined by a text where events are already finished, because they are on paper, into a creature of the present for whom events are still in the midst of forming. The actor does this by offering himself or herself not simply as one who pretends to experience premapped events but as one whom the events on stage actually change in some way as they occur. Great actors are always caught up in the adventure of allowing the play to re-create them.

On stage it is always now.

THORNTON WILDER,
THE INTENT OF THE ARTIST

REFERENCES

Centeno, Augustus, ed. *The Intent of the Artist*. Princeton, NJ: Princeton University Press, 1941. Wilder's contribution covers a lot of ground. His notion that theatrical events usually appear to be occurring in the present is relatively widespread. For example, student directors are usually told they are responsible for making the events indicated by a script "take place" on stage. On a different level, Susanne Langer echoes Wilder's notion of the theatre as a succession of present events in her philosophical study of art, *Feeling and Form*.

Jones, Robert Edmond. *The Dramatic Imagination*. New York: Theatre Arts Books, 1941.

Langer, Susanne K. *Feeling and Form: A Theory of Art*. New York: Scribner, 1953.

*(Notes, ideas,
sketches, reactions
to the exercises . . .)*

*(Notes, ideas,
sketches, reactions
to the exercises . . .)*

*(Notes, ideas,
sketches, reactions
to the exercises . . .)*

Working with Time

In the introduction to Part II, I distinguished between historical time and duration. In the theatre, the first leads to a study of period style (a subject I only touch on in this book), while the second, the focus in this chapter, has more to do with the way time feels, its sensuous and emotional side.

We become aware of time as duration in the rhythm of awakening and growing sleepy, variations in our pulse and breathing rates, the ebb and tide of our energy levels during the day, and in the arousal and waning of attention, lust, anger, and other feelings that come and go from one moment to the next. One of the brute realities of human life is that time, in some form or other, is always an issue. We can never recover the moment just past, no matter how cherished; the present is slipping away even as we live it; and the future is ever ahead, beckoning toward both a new day and eventual death.

Our sense of time is complex and can vary from one situation to the next. For example, some experiences feel longer than others, even though they may require the same amount of clock time. For me, waiting often seems to slow time down and make me anxious and irritable. Others may experience differently the time they spend waiting—for instance, as a moment of calm, a kind of vacation that passes all too quickly.

Time is no less mysterious on stage than off. In fact, it may operate with an even greater range of variation and subtlety in the world of a play than it does in our daily lives. For example, in an early scene in *Of Mice and Men,* George and his friend Lenny have some extra time on their hands. They take the opportunity to pay attention to small and large details in their relationship and to indulge in dreams of the future. But at the climax

For what is time? . . . Surely, we understand it well enough when we talk about it; we understand it also when in speaking with another we hear it named. What is time then? If nobody asks me, I know, but if I wanted to explain it to someone who asked me, plainly I do not know.

ST. AUGUSTINE,
CONFESSIONS

of the play, time becomes a constricting force. A lynch mob searches for Lenny. George finds him first and intends to help his friend escape. But Lenny's needs and the hopelessness of the situation interrupt George and force him to surrender his sense of practical urgency. He repeats once more the same dreams he and Lenny shared toward the beginning of the play. Both men occupy a brief, comforting moment of fantasy and memory outside the rushing, consequential pursuit of time, which eventually catches up to both of them, although in different ways. To play George or Lenny effectively, an actor must distinguish the kinds of impact time has on the characters at various points in the play.

As Joseph McGrath and Janice Kelly point out in *Time and Human Interaction,* all of us experience time in a number of ways. For example, sometimes it seems to "stand still"; at other times, it "flies by." Just how time feels depends on a lot of things: on what else is going on with us at a particular moment, on the makeup of our personalities, on our moods and social agendas.

Like the other given circumstances, time is always acting upon you. Your job as an actor is to sensitize yourself to the different workings of time in order to respond to it deeply and appropriately.

EXERCISES

There are four different ways of experiencing time that are particularly useful to actors. Each is really a framework or grid that shapes your awareness of time, giving it a particular sensory and psychological impact. I have labeled these temporal frameworks informally:

1. passage and limits
2. beginnings and endings
3. time in relation to other given circumstances
4. "time to" and "time for"

The exercises under each of these headings will give you the opportunity to find and develop variety in your encounters with time.

Passage and Limits

"It's later than you think" and "Finish this by . . . " are phrases that can change the acid content of your stomach and ruin the nicest day. The first attests to the impact of time-on-the-move, and the second to the power of temporal constraints. Passage and limitations go hand in hand to form one of the grids that influence the taste of time.

Exercise 8–1: Time and External Concentration

1. Ask your partner to keep time with a watch.
2. When he or she says "go," begin concentrating on something outside yourself—a stage property, a piece of clothing, something simple and ordinary.
3. Call "stop" when you think a minute has gone by. Check with your partner to compare your own subjective sense of a minute with the clock's version.

Exercise 8–2: Time and Internal Concentration

1. Repeat the exercise.
2. This time focus on an internal state (a mental image, thought, feeling, and so on).
3. Stop when you think a minute has elapsed.

Take a moment to compare the results of the last two exercises. How do external and internal concentration influence your sense of time? Which kind of concentration produces a longer minute? Which produces a shorter minute? Does either kind produce a clock minute?

Exercise 8–3: Opposite Time Constraints

1. With a partner, improvise a simple conversation. You may want to talk about something close at hand: the kind of day you are each having, your jobs, school, the weather, and so on. The subject should be easy to talk about.
2. Pretend you both have plenty of time.
3. Say "stop" when one of you thinks three minutes have passed.
4. Now improvise the same or a similar conversation as though you are each in a hurry. When one of you thinks one minute has passed, call "stop."
5. Report to one another and the rest of the class the feelings, associations, images, impulses, or feelings the exercise evoked.

Guidelines: Step 5 is the most important. Working with such opposite time constraints probably produces different kinds of inner life. You may want to repeat the exercise two or three times in order to become more fully attuned to the inner life it evokes.

Exercise 8–4: Using Time

1. Improvise a short conversation with a partner.

2. Pretend that both of you have had this conversation countless times.

3. One of you wants this to be the last time you talk about the subject and is in a hurry to end the conversation. The other is in no particular hurry and sees this as just another installment in a discussion that will probably reoccur frequently.

4. Again report whatever inner life the improv. provokes.

Exercise 8–5: Applications to the Text

1. Choose another jump or scene and memorize it.

2. Do it with a partner as though you both have plenty of time on your hands.

3. Then repeat the dialogue as though both of you are in a hurry.

4. Assume a different position and posture for each time condition (i.e., one position for when you have plenty of time, another for when you must hurry).

Exercise 8–6: Time Conflict and Text

1. Repeat your memorized dialogue twice with a partner.

2. As you repeat it a third time, pretend that you suddenly remember another important obligation. You must get to the end of the dialogue quickly but without telling your partner that you have another appointment.

3. Switch roles with your partner. Now, you are the one with enough time and he or she remembers another engagement.

Exercise 8–7: Changing Time Frames with the Text

1. Begin your memorized dialogue.

2. Pretend that both you and your partner think you are late for work or some other important appointment.

3. At a certain prearranged point, you both realize it's your day off or that the important appointment is really on another day.

Guidelines: In order to keep the exercise simple, you may want to insert a brief line or two at the point where you both realize that there is no need to hurry. For example,

A: Why are we hurrying?

B: What do you mean? . . . Oh, that's right. Today is _____ .

Beginnings and Endings

Time at the beginning of a particular endeavor or experience has a different feel from time at the end. One way to tune into your own sense of beginnings and endings is to make an associative grid:

Beginning = starting, starting up, starting over, getting ready, arriving, turning on, tuning in, new, entering, entrance, early, morning, sunrise, honeymoon, childbirth, and so on

Ending = finishing, finish line, termination, winding down, stopping, switching off, tuning out, exit, leaving, late, evening, sunset, divorce, falling apart, starting over, and so on

Before starting the next sequence of exercises, make up your own associative grid on a piece of paper. Write down your associations but do not share them with anyone else. The idea is simply to locate your own sense of beginnings and endings outside the context of any specific exercise.

Exercise 8–8: Interpersonal Time

1. Create a simple dialogue using "yes" and "no."
2. Play the "yes" character as though he or she were beginning a relationship, and the "no" character as though ending one.
3. Before beginning the dialogue, make an associative grid on the subject of beginning and ending a relationship. If you are the "yes" character, construct a grid of "beginning" words only, and vice versa.
4. Now, do the dialogue. Then switch roles and repeat the exercise again.

Exercise 8–9: Interpersonal Time and the Text

1. Do the exercise again.
2. But use your text instead of "yes" and "no."

Guidelines: You need not pretend that the words of the dialogue are the very first or last words you are speaking to one another. It is enough to think of the dialogue as coming somewhere *near* the beginning or ending of your relationship.

Time in Relation to Other Given Circumstances

The other elements of the given circumstances influence your experience of time, and time influences how you experience them. The following exercises will help you discover ways that agents, environments, events, and time affect one another.

Exercise 8–10: Time and the Other

1. Choose a character-role (see Chapter 5) that will slow down your partner. Let him or her play a character-role that will speed you up. For example, your partner might play a parent trying to get to work while you play a sick child who wants mom or dad to stay home.

2. Improvise a simple conversation. (You can use "yes" and "no" again, if you wish.)

3. After running the exercise for a minute or two, make a list of the associations, impulses, feelings that you experienced. Keep these private. Then run the exercise two or three more times.

4. Switch roles and repeat the exercise.

Exercise 8–11: Time and Environment

1. Choose a setting that will cause one of you to speed up and the other to slow down a little, such as a porch on a beautiful evening. One of you finds it romantic; the other is afraid of the dark.

2. Improvise a conversation that goes with your chosen environment.

3. As in the previous exercise, take note of your interior life.

4. Switch roles and repeat.

Exercise 8–12: Time and Event

1. Choose an event happening to both you and your partner that will speed up one of you and slow down the other. (Improvise.) For example, you are both at a bus stop. A bus arrives, and your partner believes that he alone will be boarding it. Accordingly, he must hurry his end of the conversation along. You, on the other hand, know that you too are boarding the same bus, so there is no need to hurry. Notice how the definition of the event differs: (a) The bus is separating us and (b) the bus is keeping us together.

2. Notice associations, impulses, feelings.

3. Switch roles and repeat the exercise.

Exercise 8–13: Application/Improvisation

1. Choose character-roles that speed one of you up and slow the other down.

2. Define the environment and the event with your partner in a way that supports both of your rates (fast and slow).

3. Improvise a short conversation that fits the circumstances and rates you have chosen. The following list offers some suggestions:

Possible Character-Roles:
   teacher ←→ student (don't forget to choose opposite rates)
   boyfriend ←→ girlfriend
   parent ←→ child
   master ←→ slave

Possible Environments:
   classroom
   front porch
   breakfast table
   throne room

Possible Event Outlines:
   The school day has just ended.
   You have just arrived on your girlfriend's or boyfriend's front porch
      after an evening out together.
   It's the morning after report cards have been sent out.
   Rumors of revolution have been spreading through the palace.

Exercise 8–14: Application to the Text

1. Memorize a new dialogue or use one you already know. Choose character-roles, an environment, and an event that seem to fit your memorized dialogue.

2. One of you is in a hurry. The other has lots of time.

3. Do the dialogue three or four times, or until you have comfortably assimilated the circumstances you have agreed upon.

"Time To" and "Time For"

Two broad perspectives on time are part of our general socialization. These come under the headings of "time to" and "time for." Both are really complex attitudes (i.e., networks of feelings, beliefs, preferences, and values) toward time that our culture makes available to us. In fact, these attitudes have been at work throughout this chapter and underlie most of the responses evoked by the exercises you have already done.

"Time to" presents human time as movement. Whether slow or rapid, the movement of time is incessant and irreversible. To live successfully, you must "keep pace" with time, always careful not to "fall behind." Keeping up with time means transforming daily life into a schedule of tasks: "It's time to eat." "It's time to throw out the rubbish." "It's time to pay the bills." "It's time to plant corn." "It's time to die." We experience time as movement from one task to another, or from the beginning through the middle to the end of a single task. Even relaxation becomes a task in the schedule of life: "It's 2 P.M. and time to take a nap."

A second metaphor associated with "time to" is the notion of time as some sort of precious but mysterious resource that is steadily on the decrease. Getting from one task to the next—moving with time—requires "spending time," and each expenditure brings us closer to death, when we are finally "out of time" and can no longer perform another task.

The sense of "time to" pervades the second half of *Hamlet*. After he kills Polonius, Hamlet moves systematically from one situation to another en route to avenging his father. What is more, Hamlet responds to each situation *in order to* get to the next one. Each situation takes its meaning principally from becoming part of the pathway that leads Hamlet to a showdown with Claudius. But with each aggressive response, Hamlet comes closer to using up the finite amount of time granted him by the world in which he moves.

The emotional power of living according to the tyranny of "time to" is complex. On the one hand, living on a time schedule offers us a sense of security, allowing us to structure time in relation to our desires for achievement and results. A schedule promises us at least an opportunity to get things done. On the other hand, "time to" can also evoke desperation, partially because it places us on a treadmill, where tasks are all there are and time is a sentence to hard labor, and partially because all the hard labor in the world cannot forestall the eventual depletion of time.

The attitude called "time for" views time somewhat like a still body of water—a puddle, pool, swamp, or ocean. Time does not move. Instead, we move through it. Life is a "voyage," and we are all "sailors" on the "sea" of time; death is a distant or not so distant "shore." Clichés such as these point out the pervasiveness of this particular attitude. We use the phrase "time for" as often as "time to": time for gardening, time for feeding the baby, time for dinner, and so on.

When functioning according to the rules of "time for," our sense of time is determined by the structure and quality of whatever experience we are involved in. We do not *spend time* on an experience (this is the idiom of "time to"). Instead, an experience *occupies* time. For instance "time for feeding the baby" differs from "time to feed the baby." The latter phrase suggests that a specific, predetermined amount of time has been set aside, and when that time is up, the task of feeding will come to an end and be supplanted by another task. The former phrase suggests that there is no predetermined amount of time for the baby, but that feeding will continue for as long as it takes to complete the experience or for as long as it is valuable to someone. On different days, it may take varying amounts of time.

The attitude of "time for" seems crucial to part of Laura's scene with Jim, the Gentleman Caller, in *The Glass Menagerie*. As she shows Jim her collection of glass animals, Laura's use of time is not constrained by the sense that she has only so much of it at her disposal. Showing her collection to Jim is not on a schedule. Laura functions without the anxious feeling that something must come next and call a halt to her sharing of her private life. But after the glass unicorn breaks, Laura's conversation about her figurines comes to an end. She returns to a "time to" attitude and becomes conscious that moments are passing and she needs to come up with something to say or do. We see the charming, low-key confidence of the menagerie sequence disappear and her painful uncertainty return.

"Time for" is not always so upbeat. It too can exercise a tyranny over our emotional lives, for without preset boundaries, some experiences can last "forever." Time that slows down or stands still may be as horrid as time that never stops moving. If you like feeding babies, the time it occupies may be a lovely pool where you can dangle your feet, but if you dislike bottles, sucking, and mucus, the time can become a swamp. "Time for" grieving, after a personal disaster, may suggest that grief is more than part of a schedule of emotional tasks that must be checked off one at a time, and that a space has been opened up within time expressly for grief. But the very lack of specific boundaries can make the grief harder to bear. ("When will this ever end?") Perhaps Ophelia finds her "time for anguish" so unbearable that she can escape only by taking leave of her senses and committing suicide. It is the lack of specific, predetermined temporal boundaries and the deemphasis on "getting on with it" (whatever "it" might be) that, for better or for worse, are at the crux of "time for."

The attitudes I call "time to" and "time for" can elicit a rich, though not necessarily comfortable, emotional life, but only if you confront them head on by making them part of your work in the studio and rehearsal hall. I hope the next sequence of exercises will (1) make you more aware of how both "time to" and "time for" are already at work in the way you experience your own daily life and (2) heighten the ability of both attitudes to elicit responses from you in rehearsal and performance.

Exercise 8–15: Discovering Attitudes Toward Time

1. List a few of the activities that make up your normal daily life.
2. Place "time to" or "time for" after each item on your list, depending on what sense of time it evokes in you. For example,

math class	time for (there's too much time and I'm always drowning in it)
work	time to
wash dishes	time to
gardening	time for
dancing	time for

As I work on this chapter, I can feel a bit of anxiety as the sense of "time to write" and the sense of "time for writing" collide and conflict. There are two voices, each with its own strong attitude:

Time to write:	Get it right so you can move ahead. Finish this draft of Chapter 8 by May 15; so you can finish Chapter 9 by June 15; so you can revise Chapters 1–3 by July 15; so you can send everything off to Mayfield by July 20; so you can . . .
Time for writing:	Forget your schedule. Play. Follow the ideas wherever they lead. Try to get beyond what you already know you can say clearly. Muck around in the stuff that troubles you about time and acting. Write about that. Besides, there's no future in closure.
Time to write:	This dialogue is taking too long.
Time for writing:	When you finish this section, you'll only have to go on to the next. Just ask "time to." So, why worry about finishing? For now, just write whatever.

Exercise 8–16: Subtexting Temporal Attitudes

1. Choose a simple activity you can do in front of the rest of the class—tie your shoe, brush your hair, arrange some light furniture or props, and so on.

2. Continue or repeat the activity until you can decide which attitude toward time accompanies it. Is it "time to" or "time for"? Are you worried about having to accomplish something, or about getting something done before time runs out? Or, does the sense of necessity and schedule slip away? Maybe you are absorbed in the activity in a way that pushes worry about schedule and time limits to the background of your consciousness. Perhaps you are simply revelling in being the center of attention or worrying about how you look to others.

3. When your sense of time becomes clear, let it talk to you. That is, make "time to" or "time for" a character and listen to what it says. Use its "conversation" as a subtext.

Guidelines: Remember to create the subtext while you are doing the activity. You are under no obligation to remember the subtext. Trying to remember can create a lot of unnecessary tension.

Exercise 8–17: Time/Text/Body

1. Find a physical position that helps you move into the attitude you need for your chosen text. For example, a sense of "time as a schedule" (i.e., time to) might become more accessible if you get down on all fours in the starting position for the hundred-yard dash. A "time for" attitude

might come more easily if you take your shoes off and pretend you are sitting on the side of a pool or lake or sewer with your feet in the water.

2. Now do your dialogue in your chosen position. Repeat the dialogue while gradually coming back to your normal posture. Take your time.

Exercise 8–18: Body/Movement/Text/Time

1. Find a vigorous movement that goes with the postural attitude toward time you used in the last exercise. For example,

   Time to: sprinting around the perimeter of the acting space

   Time for: splashing around or swimming or drowning in a pool of water/time

2. Spend a minute doing just the movement. (Make sure you and your partner do not collide.)

3. Now join your dialogue to the movement.

4. Keep the movement at an exaggerated level for about two minutes; then begin to reduce the size of the movement until you are in a normal position (sitting or standing). Repeat the dialogue two or three more times concentrating on one another.

Our responses to time are intimately bound up with our sense of mortality. One of the bonds that unites us is that we are all in the process of dying. Time runs out on us, or we finally finish our journey across it. Death is scary. Therefore, impasse may often occur quickly at the outset of an exercise on the theme of time. Remember, as I noted earlier, impasse in the form of boredom, confusion, giddiness, lapse of memory ("What did you say was the next step in this exercise?") is important. It helps us avoid troublesome feelings. Acknowledge it when you think it is happening and go on to the next exercise. You can always come back. Training, when it is intelligent, is often circular—a returning to what you have tried before, but a returning that is also a renewal because of the additional experience you bring back to what you have already done. Paradoxically, while our anxiety about death may cause impasse, impasse itself is not the end of a process that has failed but the beginning of a return to something important.

REFERENCES

Cottle, Thomas J., and Stephen L. Klineberg. *The Present of Things Future.* New York: The Free Press, 1974. A fairly technical discussion of the way our sense of the future influences us in the present.

McGrath, Joseph E., and Janice R. Kelly. *Time and Human Interaction*. New York: Guilford Press, 1986. A book about the various predominant descriptions of time in physics, biology, and the social sciences. One of its themes is the variety of ways human beings experience time.

McGrath, Joseph E., ed. *The Social Psychology of Time*. Newberry Park, CA: SAGE Publications, 1988. McGrath collects a number of essays about the impact of time on social interactions. Many use empirical apparatus.

*(Notes, ideas,
sketches, reactions
to the exercises . . .)*

*(Notes, ideas,
sketches, reactions
to the exercises . . .)*

(Notes, ideas, sketches, reactions to the exercises . . .)

Working Across
the Given Circumstances

*The nuances and
the color of the
actions [on stage]
will depend on the
circumstances which
provoke [them].*

SONIA MOORE,
THE STANISLAVSKI SYSTEM

The exercises presented in the last five chapters have focused on each of
the given circumstances—agents, environment, event, and time—more or
less individually. Working with the components of a dramatic situation
one at a time instills a keen sensitivity to the unique contribution each can
make to your work.

Other exercises work more broadly, encompassing several of the given
circumstances at once. Building on the sensitivities you have developed in
the previous chapters, these exercises acquire their power from the
breadth and variety of the excitation they offer. Although none of them is
very complicated, they do require that you take your time and work slowly
and deeply. Concentration, relaxation, and free breathing are your most
important tools. All three directly support your emotional life. Restricted
breathing, muscular tension, and spotty concentration are ways to shield
yourself from the emotional charge that the exercises might induce. A better protective strategy, if you need one, is simply to stop doing an exercise
that you find unsettling. Acting is not supposed to make you miserable.
Getting the training you need is not always fun, but it should contribute
to your overall sense of well-being. Joyless actors create joyless performances—something no audience needs as part of its experience in the
theatre.

The exercises selected for this chapter rely heavily on the quality of the
relationships among students. Mutual support and positive regard are
always necessary to make these exercises take root. Actors must be able to
trust one another in order to get all that they can from the work they do.

Since a thorough state of relaxation is a necessary prelude to the coming exercises, before beginning, review the following relaxation strategy, or formulate your own by selecting a few simple exercises from Part I.

1. Lie comfortably on your back with your knees up and your feet flat on the floor.
2. Set up a breathing rate a little slower than your usual one. Concentrate on breathing gently with your entire torso. (You've done this before in Part I.)
3. Find those muscle groups that feel held or tight.
4. Imagine you are inhaling into each of these muscle groups.
5. As you exhale, let go of the tension you have located.

Guidelines: Work on each of the tight muscle groups one at a time. Avoid hyperventilating by making sure that exhaling takes a little longer than inhaling.

EXERCISES

Text Association

In general, the purpose of text association is to connect the world of the text to your own personal life. This is accomplished by allowing the playwright's words to trigger private images from your own subconscious life. Done in a relaxed state, text association stimulates heightened responses to the given circumstances to which the words of a text most often refer.

Exercise 9–1: Associating from the Text

1. Memorize another scene. Then make a short list of some of the more important words spoken by your character. From three to five words should be enough.
2. Go through the relaxation procedure given above.
3. As you do so, whisper the word list to yourself, one word on each exhalation.
4. Remaining on your back with your knees up, go through your short word list again. Let each word evoke a series of one-word associations. Say them in a whisper. When you run out of associations, go to the next word on the list. There are no right or wrong associations. Use whatever comes.

5. After you've done the exercise two or three times (the associations may be different each time), sit up and repeat the exercise once more, speaking your associations aloud to another member of the class, who then shares his or her associations with you.

Guidelines: Notice that the text belongs to the character, but the associations belong to you. This exercise is yet another way of merging the self with the character.

Example of Associative Chains from
Sexual Perversity in Chicago *by David Mamet*

DANNY: You think she was a pro?

BERNARD: A pro, Dan . . .

DANNY: Yes.

BERNARD: . . . is how you think about yourself. You see my point?

DANNY: Yeah.

BERNARD: Well all right, then, I'll tell you one thing . . . she knew all the pro moves.

Word List	*Bernard's Association Chain*
"pro"	prostitute, sex, money, adventure, guilt, mother
"think"	conscience, inhibition, inadequacy, stale, trapped, terror, stuck
"knew"	new, competent, professional, responsible, exciting, sex, carnal, Bible, prostitute, robes, priest[1]

The more deeply personal your associations are the better. For this reason, step 5 may seem very uncomfortable in a classroom setting. It is better to ask to be excused from the final step rather than to force yourself to do something that violates your personal boundaries. Or, perhaps you might share just a couple of associations while saying "pass" in place of those you cannot share aloud.

Exercise 9–2: Association and Movement

1. Repeat the exercise standing up.
2. This time try to join movements with your associations, the bigger the better—one movement for each association.
3. Remember not to say your associations aloud until you have done the exercise silently two or three times.
4. In other words, the first two or three times you do the exercise you will be moving and just whispering the associations.

Exercise 9–3: Moving Back to Your Text

1. Stand in the acting space with your partner.

2. Concentrate on one another and do your dialogue.

Guidelines: The greatest injustice you can do yourself and your work is trying to remember the associations you have discovered (both movements and words). Let the normal conditioning process do the work.

Animation Sketches

Some actors strive arduously to whip up an emotional display, as though that alone constituted their performance. Treating your emotional life as a cosmetic mask is self-indulgent and exploitative. On stage, emotion is never an end in itself. Instead, it is always an animating force that charges and enlivens the rest of the world on stage. Think of your feelings as a form of life-giving electric energy and yourself as a transmitter that passes the energy on.

To animate someone or something on stage requires the body to function as a vehicle of transmission, a point the next sequence of exercises emphasizes.

Exercise 9–4: Animating Objects

1. Begin by renewing your relaxation.

2. Choose a set piece, prop, or costume that fits into the scene or jump you have chosen to memorize.

3. Using "yes" and/or "no" (you might end up shifting from one to the other), imagine you are infusing the object wih the way you feel at the moment. You may want to think of yourself as simply imparting your emotional energy to the object.

4. The attention you are paying to the object, the energy you are investing in it, and its evident connection to your emotional states are what give it a life on stage.

Exercise 9–5: Movement Animation

1. Repeat the last exercise.

2. But refrain from any vocal utterance. Instead, move the object you've chosen in whatever ways make you feel that you are truly imparting your feelings *both to and through it*. (Since feelings can change as they

are expressed, you may end up alternately jumping on and then caressing a scarf or pushing then hugging a chair.)

Guidelines: Remember, a prop or costume piece is a *means* of "expressing" (i.e., transmitting) feelings.

Exercise 9–6: Animating Others

1. This time energize another actor with your feelings, once again using "yes" and/or "no."
2. Take turns so that the exchange becomes a dialogue.
3. After twenty to thirty seconds, begin moving in a large circle, trying always to face each other from opposite sides of the circumference.
4. As your feelings and impulses change, alter the speed, shape, and intensity of your movement and vocal work.

Exercise 9–7: Animation/Text/Other

1. Renew your relaxation.
2. Repeat step 1 of the previous exercise.
3. But instead of using "yes" or "no," use two or three of the words or a short phrase from your text.
4. Once again, take turns with your partner so that the exchange becomes a dialogue uttered while circling. Remember to breathe into a loose torso. The more commitment you make to the exercise, the more your feelings, voice work, and body movement will vary from moment to moment.

Some people break pencils, kick chairs, slam doors, shout at others, or make derogatory gestures at bad drivers. All are negative ways of imparting energy to the surroundings. When we animate our own circumstances with destruction and upset, the same kind of energy comes back at us, or else we are left entirely alone. On stage you must transform your feelings and emotional power into positive forces by sharing them in a way that prods the given circumstances to change and respond back at you in a useful and lively fashion. It is this giving of the self that is the true basis of animating the world and the basis for being animated in return.

Scenes from Childhood

Scenes from our childhood provide us with potent emotional material even long after we have moved onto our adult lives. The experiences of childhood take their power, in part, from the fact that it was as children that they happened to us for the very first time. As children we experienced our first pet, our first friend, our first brush with danger, our first sense of loss—all of the stuff that makes growing up such a sad, joyous, and an altogether permanent issue. For the next exercises, I have chosen a scene-space where lots of things happened to you as a child: your bedroom.[2]

Exercise 9–8: A Room with a View

1. Relax.
2. Organize the acting space so it fits your memorized dialogue. Create the physical environment for your script carefully.
3. Explore the setting for five minutes. (Sit on the chairs or floor, stand or crawl on the platforms, play on the sofa or stool, pretend the edge of a bench is a tightrope. See how many ways you can move in the space.)
4. Now, *reorganize the space* so that you can "see" the bedroom you had as a child. (If the acting space has little or no furniture, you can furnish it with your imagination. If it contains some set pieces, transform these imaginatively into your former bedroom furniture and rearrange them appropriately.)
5. Go to where the closet would be and name the familiar items you see. Touch each one. (Consistency is not important. You might recall a dress you got at eight next to a baseball glove you received at twelve.)
6. Explore the rest of your room. What's in your chest of drawers? Go through each one slowly. Touch and describe some of their contents.

Exercise 9–9: Finding a Cherished Object

1. Find a personal object you once kept in your room.
2. Examine it and tell the class what it is. Then put it back where it belongs. Take your time. Can you remember why the object was so special to you?

Exercise 9–10: Activity and Scene-Space

1. Now, remember some very simple activity you often did in your room—cleaning, picking up clothes, looking for a lost sock, maybe playing with that cherished object you found in the last exercise.
2. Actually perform one or two of the simpler activities. Exaggerate the movement they require, perhaps even turning the movement into a dance.

Exercise 9–11: Childhood Scenes with Others

1. Imagine someone from your childhood coming into your room. It may be a friend, parent, or a sibling.
2. Ask the person why he or she has come and what he or she needs or wants from you. Listen for an answer. (Do all of this silently.)

Exercise 9–12: Back to the Text

1. Restore the space to the environment you had arranged originally for your text.
2. Now, do the last four exercises once again, this time from the point of view of your character. That is, (a) rearrange and explore the kind of room you think your character had as a child; (b) find a cherished object he or she might have used; (c) do a typical activity; (d) question someone from the character's past.
3. Leave the exercise behind and do your dialogue two or three times with your partner.

Crucial scenes occurred in other childhood spaces as well: your backyard, the grammar school playground, a nearby restaurant where your parents used to buy you cokes or ice cream cones. Any of these might have been a "stage" for an important moment in your early development and could be used as the basis of the previous five exercises.

Wishing and Imagining

Other useful sources of emotional life are occurrences and situations we *wish for* or *imagine* in our daydreams and fantasies. A home run in the bottom of the ninth with the bases loaded, auditioning and getting that first professional role, meeting someone who likes you as much as you like him or her: All of us have *wished for* and *imagined* payoffs similar to these. The next exercises attempt to splice together your own private fictions with the textual fiction of the scene or jump you are using.

Exercise 9–13: Living Biography

1. Invent three different situations involving a character or object from your text. For example, if you were cast as Laura in the scene with Jim from *The Glass Menagerie,* you might begin by imagining yourself rescuing him from drowning. Next, imagine managing a china and glass shop together. Finally, try to see a day in your life with Jim after five years of marriage.

2. In order to make the fantasies concrete, write a one- or two-page description of each one. Personalize the description by writing in the first person (I or we).

Exercise 9–14: Living the Biography

1. Ask your partner to help you improvise all three of the situations you've just invented. Keep the improvisations brief and simple. None should take more than two or three minutes.

Exercise 9–15: Back to the Text

1. Now, do your dialogue with your partner two or three times.
2. Strive to concentrate on one another rather than on preserving whatever you think you got from doing the exercises. Let the work take effect automatically.

Memory and Combined Circumstances

In addition to wishes and fantasies, actual memories can also cause different combinations of circumstances to deeply affect our emotional lives. Except for the last two steps, the following exercise is a traditional affective memory exercise.

Exercise 9–16: Memory, Voice, and Text

1. Say a line from your dialogue aloud two or three times.
2. Recall an incident from the past when you wish you had used similar words or at least expressed a similar idea.
3. Review the incident with your five senses. That is, recall what was said, the sights, smells, tactile sensations, and the taste it all left in your mouth.
4. Then begin repeating out loud the line you've selected.
5. Vary the volume and speed of the line in accordance with the feelings the recall elicits.

Exercise 9–17: Regressions

1. Take a moment to renew your relaxation.
2. Sit comfortably on the floor or in a chair and run through the lines from your dialogue with your partner.

3. Select a line, phrase, or word that seems important to you. Say it aloud to your partner two or three times.

4. Now, try to recall something that actually happened to you about a week ago. Use the first memory that comes to mind. It need not appear to fit the scene or the word(s) you have chosen. (The "fit" is a matter best left to the subconscious.)

5. Make the memory as vivid as possible by reviewing it with your five senses. What did you see, hear, taste, touch, smell?

6. When the memory becomes vivid, say your chosen line/word/phrase three or four more times out loud to your partner (or the class).

7. Now, move back in time about a month. When you have fixed on a memory and made it vivid, say your word or passage three or four times again.

8. From this point, move back in time spans of from three to six months, finding a memory and saying your lines until you work your way back three to five years.

9. End the exercise by repeating the original scene or dialogue with your partner.

Guidelines: Never use a memory that hurts you.

Synesthesia

Our responses to the given circumstances around us depend partly on the sensory channels we use to access those circumstances and how we choose to position ourselves in relationship to what our senses tell us. In general, there are at least three positions we can occupy toward our sensory input: the position of a "he" or "she," a "you," or an "I." Depending on your personality, each position will result in different reactions to the situation you are focusing on. By coupling certain sense channels (sight, hearing, and so on) with each subject position (I, you, he, she), you can alter and intensify your engagement with your surroundings. Before beginning each of the next four exercises, read through it, paying particular attention to the examples.

Exercise 9–18: Synesthesia, Third Person, Visual

1. Relax.

2. Go through your dialogue two or three times with a partner.

3. Arrange the acting space for the scene; a few pieces are all you need to suggest an environment.

4. Now stand on the edge of the environment and look at it while you narrate the plotline of the scene or jump.

5. Tell your character's story in the *third person* (he or she). Focus *only* upon what your character *sees*. For example, say you are playing Bernie in the cutting from *Sexual Perversity in Chicago* used earlier in this chapter. You would narrate Bernie's "story" in the third person using verbs like "sees," "notices," "glances"—whatever verbs you associate with sight. Your narration might incorporate what you know about the context of the scene from having read the whole play. (Including details from context is not a requirement, just a natural tendency.) For example,

> "He (i.e., you-as-Bernie) sees Dan staring at him across the cocktail table. He notices Dan is so wrapped up in his tale of sex and carnage that he hasn't bothered to drink much of his beer."

> "He sees Dan's eyes fill with wonder and he notices how others in the bar are looking his way, no doubt wishing they could hear the story that Danny has found so riveting."

> "He sees Danny's eyes widen to the profundity of what he is hearing from the lips of his friend."

[handwritten margin note: As if you are talking about Briseis and what she is seeing & seeing]

Exercise 9–19: Synesthesia, Second Person, Aural

[handwritten margin note: As if you are talking about Briseis about what she hears]

1. Repeat the exercise. This time tell the story of your character in the *second person*, imagining all that he or she hears. Don't let this degenerate into merely repeating what other characters say.

2. The example here is the same cutting from Mamet's play, and the narrative is one that the actor playing Bernie might use.

> "You hear Danny's fingers stroking the table, a nervous habit. You hear him inhale each new detail that you provide."

> "Other sounds of the bar have receded. But you can still hear an occasional voice whispering in admiration of your wit and humor."

> "You hear the complete admiration and trust in Danny's voice as he says his final 'yeah.'"

> "You listen to yourself to make sure your voice falls into that fatherly manner that makes Danny's eyes shine with wonder and appreciation."

> "Ah, Bernie, Bernie—you've done it again."

[handwritten note: Energy derived from motion ———— Impulse toward movement]

Exercise 9–20: Synesthesia, First Person, Kinesthetic

[handwritten margin note: What you are feeling: feeling as in • sensations hot cold • movement]

1. This time *enter the environment you have arranged and walk* about as you do the rest of the exercise. Narrate in the *first person* whatever you think your character is feeling. The feelings may be sensations (hot,

cold, nausea, light-headedness, and so on), or they may be emotions (anger, embarrassment, elation, and so on). For example,

"I feel relieved and elated by Danny's attention."

"I'm calmer now that I've got Danny watching me rather than ogling all the women in this bar. The prospect of having to talk to a girl makes me nervous."

"I can't breathe just thinking about it."

"I feel victorious and on top of things when Danny utters his final 'yeah.'"

"I'm confident enough now to try talking to a woman. Yeah, I feel like giving it a shot."

Exercise 9–21: Synesthetic Improvisation

1. Repeat the exercise once more.
2. This time shift freely among first, second, and third persons. Change the sense channels randomly from sight to sound to touch (feeling). Just let yourself go. No need to be careful.
3. You may do the exercise while standing on the edge of the space or as you walk through the scene. For example,

"I'm worried and I need Danny's attention to reassure me. He likes my story. You could keep Dan on the edge of his seat all day."

"I'm not really afraid to meet girls. A guy like me just doesn't like singles' bars."

"You can get better action other places, like at church functions."

"No one expects a guy to come on in a church basement."

"I'm glad Danny is listening. He makes me relax. Girls like guys to be relaxed. You're on top of things now, big fella."[3]

The exercise assigns you no performance obligation. Moreover, there is no right or wrong result. As you rehearse a play or scene, your monologues will change. The exercises serve a variety of functions: (1) They drench each of your senses in the sensations available in the situation; (2) they help you translate the character's responses into your own words (his or her story gradually becomes your story); (3) the variations in point of view (he or she, you, I) empower the given circumstances to evoke a variety of potentially useful responses to the same segment of text.

There is no need to be clever or original. Say whatever comes to mind as long as it conforms to the rules of the exercise. Your statements need not be consistent. *Self-contradiction is part of the process,* especially early on when you are still finding out how the given circumstances might be working on your character.

Exercise 9–22: Back to the Text

1. Pretend the exercises happened long ago or that they never happened at all, and turn your attention outward toward your partner.

Because they are designed to address more than one of the given circumstances simultaneously, most of the exercises in this chapter are especially versatile. That is, you can alter the exercises to emphasize different combinations of circumstances. For instance, you can build a text association exercise in which you allow the words of the text to trigger only images of people and places. Or, you can recombine the elements of the synesthesia exercises (perspective and sensory channel) in different ways: (e.g., first person + sight; second person + feeling; third person + hearing). The temporal interval in the regression exercises may be shortened or widened. In addition, the object of your recall can also change. Instead of an event that happened to you, you may wish to fix on a person you met or an object you acquired. The possibilities for variation are vast. The closer you get to the exercises in this chapter the more opportunities you will find for changing them to suit your own changing needs.

A central theme in your work over the last six chapters has been the constant vulnerability that must become a normal part of your life in the theatre. It is this ready responsiveness to the who, what, where, and when of a situation that makes acting a mode of involvement in the world on stage rather than a self-exploitative routine intended only to pander to the audience.

Vulnerability is not self-victimization. Embracing the world need not reduce you to a quivering hulk of protoplasm full of uncontrollable primal impulses. Your deepened sensitivity to the given circumstances is something you yourself have created and can control. By using the exercises, you are learning how to empower your surroundings to engender outgoing responses in yourself. When everything is going well, your work with the given circumstances catches you up in a never-ending dance. In the idiom of Fred and Ginger, it is both selfish and selfless—a dance in which you receive in order to give and give in order to receive.

NOTES

1. Association exercises are attributed to both Strasberg and Stanislavski.
2. I got the idea for this exercise from my colleague, Jack Wright.
3. I owe the assumptions underlying the last five exercises to neurolinguistic programming and to Chapter 12 in Clive Barker's *Theatre Games*.

REFERENCES

Bandler, Richard, and John Grinder. *The Structure of Magic I.* Palo Alto, CA: Science and Behavior Books, 1975. An introduction to neurolinguistic programming by the authors who formulated it. While not directly about acting, the book provided many of the assumptions on which the exercises in this chapter are based.

————. *The Structure of Magic II.* Palo Alto, CA: Science and Behavior Press, 1976. This book is particularly good at describing some of the ways human beings transform sensory inputs into behavioral outputs—that is, how a stimulus becomes a response.

Barker, Clive. *Theatre Games.* New York: Drama Book Specialists, 1977. A classic in acting pedagogy. More than a compendium of exercises, *Theatre Games* offers discussions of why games and exercises are such effective means of actor training. Barker ends up sketching the outlines for a psychology of acting. Chapter 12, "Theatre Narrative and the Tenses of Acting" was particularly useful in the development of this chapter.

Moore, Sonia. *The Stanislavski System.* New York: The Viking Press, 1965 [first printed in 1960].

(Notes, ideas, sketches, reactions to the exercises . . .)

_____

_____

_____

_____

_____

_____

_____

_____

_____

_____

_____

_____

_____

_____

_____

_____

_____

_____

_____

*(Notes, ideas,
sketches, reactions
to the exercises . . .)*

*(Notes, ideas,
sketches, reactions
to the exercises . . .)*

Action, Motives, Obstacles, and Stakes

THE IMPORTANCE OF ACTION

An action is any behavior directed toward a goal. For example, when Hamlet stabs Claudius, the goal is obviously to kill him; and when Oedipus threatens Tiresias, it is to make the old prophet tell all he knows about the murder of Laius. The goals of Hamlet and Oedipus come grounded in human desire. Actions are what characters do to one another (and sometimes to things) in order to get what they want.

In the classical and modern traditions, human actions are important for a number of reasons: First, they help to establish and clarify character. Second, they are the basic building blocks of plot.

Character and Action

Some acting teachers are fond of saying (and saying repeatedly) that "characters are their actions," or that "a character is the sum total of everything he or she does." These may be overstatements, but they are useful for pointing out the close connection between action and character. For example, we get to know Willy Loman (in Death of a Salesman*) by what he does to and/or for others. In* Waiting for Godot, *we come to sense the desperation of Didi and Gogo by the way they pursue their actions, which usually have something to do with killing time and playing games. Clarity of action is the actor's greatest asset for making a character understandable.*

Plot and Action

A dramatic plot is usually made up of a series of actions performed by characters who inhabit the world of the play. Plot actions are usually connected to one another in some way—often by cause and effect (e.g., the plays of Chekhov), but sometimes by association (e.g., Megan Terry's Comings and Goings *or any of a number of performance art works). If actions have no inferable connection to one another, then there is probably no discernible plot, but rather a series of disjointed exchanges between characters.*

The theatre is not the only medium to use action to tell a story. Novels also present plots in terms of human deeds. Yet, as Susanne Langer points out, the actions of characters in a novel usually seem to have been completed in the past. For example, Ishmael, Melville's narrator in Moby Dick, *tells us about the actions of his shipmates only* after *all of their deeds have come to naught. (Even when a novelist writes in the present tense, it is generally called the "historical present.") But in the theatre, actions are most often unfolding in the present even as they are being performed by living actors.*

Playing Actions

THE PRAGMATICS OF ACTION: TWO APPROACHES

Perhaps the best way to begin working on action is to view it in terms of your previous work with the given circumstances. Whereas the given circumstances are what act upon you, actions are whatever you do to act upon the given circumstances. If the overall purpose of the given circumstances is to provoke outgoing responses, then the aim of action is to give those responses a precise shape and mission within the world of the play. Most often that mission is to bring some concrete and immediate benefit to the character you are playing. Actions, then, transform the basic energy you derive from each moment into specific behaviors, such as glaring, staring, shouting, whispering, pounding the table, or arching your eyebrows. The general purpose of these behaviors is to make the fictional world produce whatever your character wants or needs.

Different teachers view action differently. So, during the course of your training, you will probably come across several ways to incorporate action into your work. What follows are two of the more common approaches, together with variations of each.

The first defines action as whatever your character is doing to someone (or something) within a specific segment of the text. The model for this approach is simple enough:

A human being is made out of seven dollars worth of chemicals and a story. It's the story that makes the difference.

TED JOHNSON, 1989

In most traditional plays, actions both produce the world and are produced by it; so that any given action is also a reaction and vice versa.

175

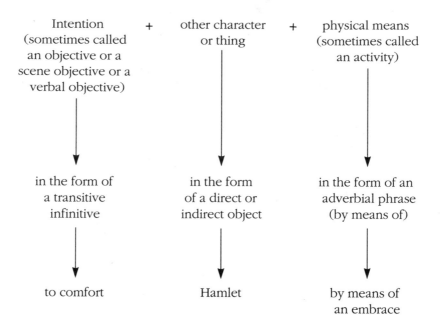

Intention   +   other character   +   physical means
(sometimes called   or thing   (sometimes called
an objective or a   an activity)
scene objective or a
verbal objective)

in the form of   in the form   in the form of an
a transitive   of a direct or   adverbial phrase
infinitive   indirect object   (by means of)

to comfort   Hamlet   by means of
                                                an embrace

This action may describe what Gertrude is doing in the bedroom scene just before the exit of the king's ghost ("O gentle son,/Upon the heat and flame of thy distemper/Sprinkle cool patience"). The transitive infinitive is crucial, for action is a transmission of energy from you directly to another. "To *be* comforting" is not a useful intention because it is a passive infinitive and cannot target someone or something that you are trying to influence or change. Moreover, the passive voice promotes a still-life approach to acting which turns each moment into a portrait of frozen energy that is used to depict a static state of being. In acting, the passive voice tends to promote showing rather than doing. The image that best represents the transitive energy pattern that your intention is supposed to capture is a simple straight arrow:

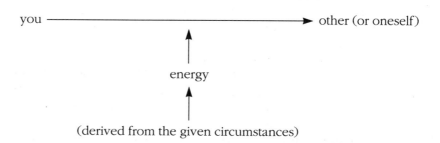

you ————————————————▶ other (or oneself)

energy

(derived from the given circumstances)

Two questions will help you use this first model: "What am I trying to do to the other character?" and "What physical means am I using to do it?"

What your character is trying to do is linked closely to the pressures of the given circumstances, as noted in the arrow diagram above, as well as to personal motivation (which will be discussed in the next chapter). Most characters do not act in a vacuum. Something from their internal and/or external worlds acts upon them in a way that makes them act back.

The physical means of achieving an intention is often called an *organizing behavior.* In the action "to comfort by means of an embrace," the physical act of embracing actually organizes the actor's body. All of the physical work you do, however subtle or expansive, must always be the means to an intention. Moreover, when a director gives you specific blocking or business, he or she is really determining means to which you must attach specific infinitives, in order to make whole actions. Sitting, standing, crossing, drinking, eating, sewing, dancing, and so on, on stage—all must become the physical means to doing something to someone or some object or, in certain cases, to oneself.

Since certain sorts of costumes and props sponsor particular kinds of movement (and physical organization), they too must be regarded as part of the means of achieving scene objectives. Fans, snuff boxes, swords, coffee mugs, cigarettes, knickers, codpieces, double-hooped skirts, and so on are all the tools a character uses to pursue intentions.

The second approach to action views it as an attempt to get someone to do something to or for you. The model looks like this:

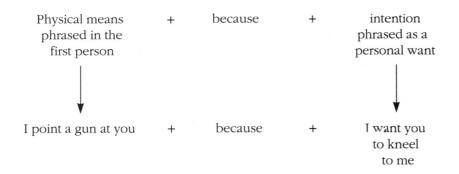

Physical means phrased in the first person	+	because	+	intention phrased as a personal want
↓				↓
I point a gun at you	+	because	+	I want you to kneel to me

The energy pattern for this approach to action is like a boomerang:

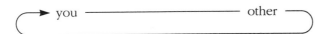

The key idea is that you want something to come back at you from the other actor/character: "I cry because I want you to hug me" or "I wrinkle my nose and puff out my cheeks because I want you to smile at me." One way to find your way into this second model is to ask the questions, "What do I want the other actor/character to do *to* or *for* me?" and "What physical behavior am I going to use to make him or her do it?"

Both of the models just sketched are really blueprints or maps for pursuing goals. All of us carry such maps throughout our everyday lives—however unconsciously—in order to help us perform the actions that will enable us to survive or enhance our well-being. But unlike most of us, actors are unusually deliberate and conscious about choosing actions for their characters. Moreover, their training makes them able to implement a particularly wide variety of action-maps. The actions of a skilled actor are efficacious, potent, penetrating, compelling, and just plain powerful.

Each of the models has its own advantages. The first requires fewer words and is therefore simpler. It also underscores the fact that one of your most important jobs on stage is to confront your partner in an attempt to influence him or her. The second explicitly connects your own physical behavior to the physical behavior you desire from the other character: "I *smile* because I want you to *smile* back at me." Such a phrasing has the advantage of making the other actor's body the precise target for your own work and emphasizes the body-to-body nature of so much worthwhile acting.

Neither approach is better or more correct than the other. Your own sensitivities, the play you are performing, and the people you are working with will help determine which of the models you use.

It is also important to recognize that both models allow you the leeway to work in a variety of ways. For example, if given the choice, some actors like to determine their transitive infinitives first and let their physical means evolve gradually by trial and error. Others prefer to predetermine at least some of the business and movement they are going to use. Phrases like "from the inside out" and "from the outside in" are often used informally to characterize these two ways of working with actions. But notice that both of the models will allow you to work however you wish.

Most important, there is a big difference between using a particular approach and letting the approach use you. A model is not supposed to be a straitjacket. Great actors learn to bend what they know to suit their own needs and the conditions in which they are working. For example, some actors like to verbalize their actions around the phrase "make you"—for example, "I smile, in order to *make you* smile at me." Some like to think of their actions as operating directly on the feelings of the other actor/character—for instance, "to make you *feel happy* by standing on my head." Other actors prefer to phrase intentions by using physical analogies, such as "to kick you," or "to spit in your face." Such analogies supply physical images that promote a certain shape and tone in the actor's expenditure of energy.

The above paragraph shows that there are many variations to both models. Before you go on to discover or invent your own, however, you will need to work with the models as they stand until you have made them second nature.

EXERCISES

Using the Models

The first set of exercises is simply to help you become adept at making action-maps according to the two approaches just explained. Making an action-map is a way of defining exactly what your character is doing or wants in each portion of the text. In fact, actions provide one way of dividing up a text. The term *beat* developed in part as a way of analyzing actions in play scripts. Whenever the action of one or more characters changes, the beat changes. Beats can vary widely in length. Here is an example from the first scene of *Hamlet*.

Scene I. Elsinore. A platform before the castle.

[*Francisco at his post. Enter to him Bernardo.*]

BER.: Who's there?

FRAN.: Nay, answer me. Stand, and unfold yourself.

BER.: Long live the King!

FRAN.: Bernardo?

BER.: He.

FRAN.: You come most carefully upon your hour.

BER.: 'Tis now struck twelve. Get thee to bed, Francisco.

Distinguishing beats is a matter of interpretation, but it is possible to think of the first two lines as constituting one beat—moreover, a beat in which both characters are pursuing the same action. Both Bernardo and Francisco are trying to elicit reassurance from the other (I want you to reassure me). They want reassurance because there is a ghost on the prowl. Both use means that come from their professions—namely, the brusque, authoritative vocal patterns of guards on alert and a shift into a stance from which they can either attack or defend. But this action performed by both characters is completed after just two lines. Bernardo's line, "Long live the King!," probably begins a new beat because Bernardo has changed his action to something such as "to put Francisco at ease." Saying "long live the King" while the dead king is roaming about could be delivered as a consciously ironic joke. (There is no need to portray these guards as stupid or witless.) So, the means might be a lighter tone of voice together with a buffoonish salute of some sort.

Exercise 10–1: Model Preference

1. Pick a jump from the appendix. Define the action of each character in terms of model 1.
2. Then define their actions according to model 2.
3. Notice which approach comes more easily to you.
4. Use both models on a few more jumps or scenes (perhaps some of those you have already worked on) until you become adept at identifying actions.

Exercise 10–2: Eavesdropping

1. Go to a restaurant, park, or any place where people congregate and talk.
2. Overhear a conversation and write it down. Ten to twelve lines should be enough. (If the conversation is so personal that listening in would be an act of disrespect, move on. Look for a simple, casual conversation. Remember, always be courteous and humane.)
3. Now repeat the last exercise by identifying the actions in the overheard dialogue according to both paradigms.
4. In this case, the organizing behaviors that make up the physical means to each action will be the actual physical activities "performed" by the people you overheard. These may be subtle and include small adjustments of posture and voice inflection.
5. Speculate about what sort of physical/vocal means may have better helped the individuals you watched go after their intentions.
6. With your partner, memorize the conversation you recorded and enact it using the revised means you've decided upon.
7. Repeat the dialogue three or four times or until it becomes fluid.

Guidelines: This exercise will help you examine the normal social means (behaviors) people use to pursue their intentions. It will also help you discover more effective behaviors.

An action-map is really a succinct statement of your commitment during a particular beat of a performance. It is a promise of what you will offer to your partners on stage no matter what. To play an action is to challenge another actor and give him or her something to react to. Actions establish what characters find nonnegotiable, over which there can be no compromise. (If a character does compromise or negotiate, it is usually a sign of defeat.) Therefore, actions form the boundaries that keep actors/characters separate and individual, and prevent their contact with one another from collapsing into the sentimental social accommodation mentioned in Chapter 5.

From Intention to Means and Vice Versa

Instead of trying to conceive of an entire action all at once, it is sometimes easier to start with half, then work gradually, through trial and error, toward the other half—for example, to start with an intention, then work toward a means or vice versa.

Whether you work from intention to means or means to intention is partially a matter of personal preference. However, you must also consider how other actors are working as well as the overall rehearsal routine. (As noted earlier, some directors lay in lots of business and staging [i.e., means] earlier in the rehearsal process. Others let the characters' physical activities develop gradually.) The next exercises will give you practice in constructing actions from both directions.

Exercise 10–3: Discovering Means

1. Supply the missing means for the following intentions:

   to comfort you by means of _____.

   I _____ because I want you to laugh at me.

2. Begin by repeating the intention three or four times out loud. Then try to *see* or *feel* yourself actually performing the intention. Fantasize freely. Whatever behavior you see or feel yourself using is the means you should state or write down.

3. There is no need to come up with logical or realistic behaviors. Allow your imagination full sway.

4. Now perform the organizing behaviors for each intention several times. Spend three to four minutes repeating each of the two movement patterns.

Exercise 10–4: Discovering Intentions

1. This time invent an intention that goes with the following organizing behaviors:

   to _____ by means of an icy stare.

   I sneer because I want you to _____ me.

   to _____ by means of a silly grin.

   I raise my hand because I want you to _____ me.

2. Before doing so, though, perform each physical means several times until an intention comes to you by association. It is important to exaggerate your physical work.

Exercise 10–5: Building Action from the Text, Intention to Means

1. With a partner, choose and memorize a dialogue from the appendix.

2. Select an intention that goes with your lines.

3. Repeat the dialogue a couple of times with the intention in mind.

4. Find a simple movement that you associate with the intention. Any motion will do as long as you feel it expresses your intention.

5. Once again the movement need not be realistic or practical.

6. Exaggerate the movement and repeat it from time to time during your own lines.

7. Gradually reduce the size of your organizing behavior until it is more realistic.

8. Then repeat the dialogue a few more times, allowing your physical means to become more or less unconscious as you focus more on your partner.

Exercise 10–6: Building Action from the Text, Means to Intention

1. Select a different text, maybe one you have used in a previous chapter. Refresh your memory by running lines with your partner a few times.

2. Each of you find a spot in the acting space that makes you feel most powerful.

3. Place yourself in a position or posture that enhances that feeling of power or control.

4. Now each of you find a simple movement that further contributes to your sense of power.

5. Repeat your movements back and forth as a dialogue with one another, without the text.

6. After two or three minutes, add to the movement the script you have memorized.

7. Continue the text until an intention occurs by association. If one does not come naturally, change your movement. If this does not help, just guess at an intention that might go with your movement.

8. Once again, continue the movement, reducing its size after your intention has become clear.

Guidelines: Try to avoid judging your work in the exercise. Neither the physical movement nor the intention needs to be perfect. You are still getting used to composing action through the use of exercises. You can always repeat the exercise if you are dissatisfied with the results.

Core Statements

Embedded in any intention is a core statement. A core statement is a phrase that turns your intention into a direct statement to the other actor/character. The statement might be a command, a plea, a hope, or a wish. For example:

Intention: "I want you to kneel to me"

Command: Kneel!

Plea: Please kneel to me.

Hope: I hope you kneel to me.

Wish: I wish you would kneel to me.

Intention: "to amuse"

Command: Laugh, damn it!

Plea: Please laugh at my jokes.

Hope: I sure hope you laugh at my jokes.

Wish: I wish you would laugh at my jokes.

Exercise 10–7: Core Dialogue

1. Run the jump or scene you are using with your partner a few times, just to refresh your memory.
2. Choose an intention. It may be one you have already used for previous exercises.
3. Transform your intention into a core statement (command, plea, hope, wish) to say to your partner. *Use the form that stands the best chance of getting through to the other actor/character.*
4. Put the text aside and carry on a dialogue with your partner using whatever form of the core statement you have chosen. Just repeat your statements back and forth.
5. Continue for three or four minutes. Depending on what discoveries you make, you may want to change the form of your core statement (from, say, a command to a plea).

Exercise 10–8: Discovering Means

1. Resume the previous exercise.
2. After two or three minutes, add a gesture or movement that expresses your core statement.
3. Exchange core statements and movement for two or three minutes, varying the size and intensity of your work.
4. Gradually, make your work more realistic.

5. Continue your dialogue, allowing the movement to become less conscious. Concentrate on your partner.

Exercise 10–9: Back to the Text

1. Start this exercise where you just left off, exchanging movement and core statements.
2. After one or two minutes, drop the core statements and use the text you and your partner have agreed to use.
3. Vary the size and intensity of your work as you repeat your lines.

Voice and Words

The human voice is an important part of most theatre productions, crucial in creating the impressions to which the audience responds. In general, it is best to regard your voice as part of the means your character uses to realize an action. The voice most often accompanies other physical means, but in some cases it may become a primary organizing behavior (that which determines the rest of the body's efforts). Here are two examples of action-maps that feature the voice:

"to comfort by means of warm, mellow tones"

"I scream because I want you to fear me"

When an actor merely puts his or her voice on display, separate from any specific intention, the result is artificial and empty—a "beautiful" sound, perhaps, but one that is without point or purpose and that makes no contribution to a character's efforts to do or get.

Since actors typically use their voices to utter words, it is crucial to recognize that language must also be part of goal-oriented behavior. When words come detached from the attempt to act upon the world of the play, the result is usually a terminal case of recitation.

Exercise 10–10: Sounds as Means

1. Recall the intention you are pursuing in the dialogue you have memorized.
2. To refresh your memory you may want to run lines with your partner once or twice.
3. Now drop the lines and exchange dialogue made of nonsense sounds (la-la-la, ba-ba-ba, k-k-k-k).
4. The sounds you choose are the means to your intention, so you may wish to experiment with a variety of sounds until you find one that seems to fit best.

5. Continue the dialogue for about two minutes, then begin moving randomly in the space. Use movement that fits the sounds you are making.

Exercise 10–11: Dialogue Sounds

1. Go back to the lines of your dialogue.
2. Choose two or three sounds (syllables) from your lines.
3. Make a dialogue with your partner, making sure to think of the sounds as means to your intentions.
4. After two minutes, find a movement or gesture that goes with the sounds.
5. Continue the dialogue for two or three more minutes, incorporating the movement.

Exercise 10–12: Text as Sound

1. Repeat the last exercise, this time using the entire words from which you just selected sounds.
2. Do a dialogue of one-word exchanges with your partner. Then begin moving freely in a way that makes the words feel more effective—that is, capable of influencing the other actor.
3. Continue the exercise for roughly three or four minutes.

Exercise 10–13: Back to the Text

1. Now, "forget" the last three exercises and do your entire dialogue. Remind yourself of the intentions you are playing.
2. Repeat the dialogue for three or four minutes, concentrating more and more on one another and on freeing yourself from any sense of obligation "to get something out of" the exercises.

Guidelines: There is no need to worry about movement. Whatever occurs is fine. Whatever special qualities your vocal work takes on, however subtle, are the primary means to your intention.

Similes and Vocal Means

One way to personalize your vocal means is by using physical similes. For example, instead of "to comfort by means of mellow, soft tones," you might use "to comfort with sounds *like* soft caresses." In the last set of exercises you may have used sounds and words like broadswords or like rapiers or perhaps like gentle, encouraging pats on the back.

Similes clarify the connection between sound and action. This clarification is particularly useful in texts that require a heightened or specialized use of the voice—for example, the plays of Shakespeare in which voice and language are invested with the power to change the lives of individual characters and the fortunes of nations.

Exercise 10–14: Warming Up the Voice-Body Connection

1. Choose a dialogue you have used previously in this chapter.
2. Recall the scene objective you've chosen to play.
3. In light of that objective, pick an entire word in each of your lines that you want to stress. (This is your "action word." If you aren't sure which word to choose, pick a verb.)
4. Run the dialogue. Every time you come to one of your chosen words leave it out and replace it with a simple but definite movement. *The bigger the better.*
5. Repeat the exercise until you become comfortable with the brief moment of silence in each line.

Guidelines: This exercise is a warm up for the next four. The movement you choose can be the same throughout the exercise, or it can vary. The more of your body the movement involves the better.

Exercise 10–15: Vice versa

1. Resume the exercise.
2. This time when you come to your chosen word in each line, say it but leave out the movement(s) you used in the last exercise.
3. The energy from the movement in the last exercise should get into the action word.

Exercise 10–16: From Movement to Verbal Simile

1. In light of the last two exercises, ask yourself, "How do I want the language to work?" Begin your answer with "like"—for example, "like a kick in the shins" or "like a pat on the cheek."
2. Now do the dialogue with your partner. When you get to the word you want to stress, leave it out and perform the simile you have chosen. (Keep the rest of the words in each line.)
3. Repeat the exercise until it becomes fluid and you are satisfied with the physical simile you have chosen.

Guidelines: Make sure to be courteous to your partner. It's all right to make violent movements in his or her direction (if your simile is a violent one). But be sure not to actually make any physical contact.

Exercise 10–20: Co...

1. Convert one of the in... ffs, NJ: Prentice-Hall, 1986
   statement (a commar... etti's book comes close to
2. Make the statement c... Nearly all of us have read
3. As you do so, use one... Chapters 19 and 20 offer
   to "back up your stat...
4. After one or two min... York: Theatre Books, 1969
   same core statement. ...ed with introducing Stan-
   ...ion of action in Chapter 3
5. Switch and let your ...ents, including Benedetti's

...field Publishing Co., 1978.

Exercise 10–21: Dia...o actions under the term

1. You and your partne...inehart, and Winston, 1966
2. Convert them to cor...Chapters 19 and 20.
3. Each of you choose ...
4. Now do a dialogue r...
   have chosen as the ...
   another.
5. Continue the exercis...
   sity of your work va...
6. After you become fan...
   your work until you ...
   and intensity for you...
7. You can repeat the e...
   statements and/or pr...

Exercise 10–22: Bac...

1. Return to the text yo...
2. Choose an intention. ...
3. Repeat the dialogue ...
   costume pieces with ...
4. Try to use the object...

Guidelines: On the fi...
other a cane. On the sec...
pieces. See how each i...
individual objectives.

(Notes, ideas,
sketches, reactions
to the exercises . . .)

(Notes, ideas, sketches, reactions to the exercises . . .)

---

*(Notes, ideas,
sketches, reactions
to the exercises . . .)*

_____

_____

_____

_____

_____

_____

_____

_____

_____

_____

_____

_____

_____

_____

_____

_____

_____

_____

_____

_____

_____

Motivating Action

Motive is one of many words in the English language known for its promiscuity. Like *love, justice,* and *liberty,* the term *motive* can be defined in ways too numerous to review. Sometimes it seems to mean just about whatever anyone wants it to. For the sake of clarity, I find it useful to define a motive as a *past and/or future event, along with the need it creates in the present.* Notice that according to this definition, a motive has two parts: (1) a past and/or future event and (2) a present need. Both parts together are what make a complete motive. For example, a childhood fraught with frequent episodes of criticism (past events) might produce a present need for continual approval from others. Or, an upcoming job interview (future event) might evoke a need for encouragement from a friend.

Recall that early scene in *The Glass Menagerie* when Amanda is out on the landing of her tenement apartment looking for Tom. What motivates her incessant calling? One motive begins in the past. Her husband has abandoned her to join the Merchant Marines. Amanda's present need is for reassurance that she has not been abandoned again—this time by her son. A second motive might come from the future. She expects that Laura will continue to burden her with a host of responsibilities that she cannot bear alone. So, Amanda needs a guarantee of economic survival that only Tom's presence can give her. Given these two motives, the actor playing Amanda might choose to call Tom's name into the night with a voice tinged by desperation and fear. Just how much desperation and fear is a matter for experimentation and discussion with the director.

The question I have to ask myself, as an actor, is no longer merely "What do I want and how do I go after it?" but "What makes me want what I want?"

JOSEPH CHAIKIN,
THE PRESENCE OF THE ACTOR

MOTIVE AS PREDISPOSITION

Motivation is particularly important to an actor because it creates two kinds of predispositions in a character. First, *a motive shapes how a character actually experiences and feels about the given circumstances going on in the present.* For instance, consider a character who has been the victim of a childhood full of parental criticism (past event) and consequently *needs* lots of approval. He or she might be predisposed to hear a boss's dissatisfaction (given circumstance) as a repetition of that original parental voice and to reexperience all those old childhood feelings of inadequacy.

Second, *a motive predisposes a character to choose a certain action in response to the given circumstances.* The character beset with the boss's criticism (given circumstance) might feel predisposed *to escape by running from the office* (action) the way he or she ran from the room as a child.

APPLYING MOTIVATION TO DRAMATIC SITUATIONS

The previous discussion will be easier to apply if we keep in mind the following procedures and examples:

A. *Motives Beginning in the Past*
   1. Capture the past event as a simple statement of what has already happened to the character you are playing prior to the beat you are working on.
   2. It helps to place yourself as the object of a transitive verb in the past tense.
      For example: My husband left me. (Amanda on the landing) My math teacher flunked me. (part of the motivation that brings Biff to Willy's hotel room in *Death of a Salesman*)

B. *Motives Beginning in the Future*
   1. Phrase the future event as an expectation: "I expect . . ."
      For example: I expect that Tom will leave me. (Amanda) I expect that flunking math will keep me out of college. (another part of what motivates Biff's fateful visit to his father's hotel room)

C. *Present Needs*
   1. Now ask yourself, "What need(s) does the past or future event produce in the character I am playing?"
   2. Let the answer be as succinct as possible, such as "I need my father" or "I need a warm hug." Remember to express the need as a noun: "my father," "a hug." The more specific it is the better.

3. Use words that are visceral. For example, "I need rescue" is a more provocative wording than, say, "I need help."

Let's put all the pieces together, focusing on Biff's motivation in the hotel scene:

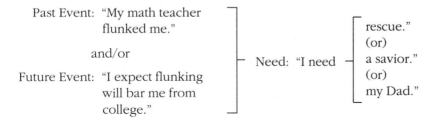

Past Event: "My math teacher flunked me."

and/or

Future Event: "I expect flunking will bar me from college."

Need: "I need

rescue."
(or)
a savior."
(or)
my Dad."

EXERCISES

Putting Motives into Words

These first few exercises are intended to help you identify motives in a comfortable and useful language. As you do the exercises, try to notice that many of your decisions about motivation are based to some extent on your ability to infer, imagine, and otherwise fill in details that are not actually mentioned in the text.

Exercise 11–1: Choosing Motives

1. Choose a scene from the appendix or use one assigned in class.
2. Pick the character you want to work on
3. Outline in general terms what seems to be going on in the scene. To focus your thoughts, ask yourself:
   a. What is the scene about?
   b. What contribution does my character make to whatever is going on? (The purpose of these questions is simply to get you thinking about the overall context of the scene in a way that will make finding motives a little easier.)
4. Now, answer the following questions specifically about motivation:
   a. What event from the past and/or future seems to be working on your character?
   b. What need or needs does the event bring on?

Exercise 11–2: Motivation and Interpretation

1. Repeat the exercise but try to find or invent a different event and need.

2. How does the new motive alter the way you see your character from the way you viewed him or her in the first exercise?

From Event to Needs

The goal of the next exercises is to help you translate past and future events into deep personal needs. Since the process of need formation is gradual, the sequence of the next eight exercises is particularly important.

Exercise 11–3: Visualizing a Past Circumstance

1. Choose a scene and memorize it with a partner.

2. Find or invent a past circumstance that might serve as part of your character's motivation. (When you are working with an entire script, your choices will be based on the whole text and the director's interpretation.) Do not worry about a future circumstance or a need yet.

3. Try to *see* what it was that happened to your character.

4. Report what you see to your partner or the class as it occurs in your imagination.

5. Now let your partner do the exercise.

Guidelines: Make your report in the first person, as if you were the character.

Exercise 11–4: Hearing the Past

1. Use the same past circumstance.

2. This time report everything your character *heard*.

Exercise 11–5: Investing the Past with Feelings

1. Now, report the *feelings* your character remembers experiencing in the past circumstance you are using.

Exercise 11–6: Discovering Needs

1. Run the scene you have chosen with your partner two or three times.

2. In light of the last three exercises, choose a need that seems to arise out of the sights, sounds, and feelings you have imagined.

3. Phrase the need(s) simply. You might try using short sentences such as "I need sympathy," or "I need warmth." If you think several needs are operating simultaneously, you can join them—for example, "I need sympathy and a hug." The idea is to keep your need statements as concrete as possible. Remember to use nouns.

4. Repeat the dialogue you have memorized two or three times with your partner. Try to concentrate on one another, allowing your work in the last four exercises to transfer without any special attention on your part.

Guidelines: Notice that defining needs can bring you close to choosing an action. If your character needs warmth, maybe his or her intention is: "I want you to hug me."

Exercise 11–7: Visualizing the Future

1. Using the same scene, think of a future event (expectation) that is influencing your character.

2. Visualize the event as though it were actually happening to you in the here and now.

3. Complete the exercise by reporting what you see.

4. Now switch and allow your partner to do the exercise.

Exercise 11–8: Hearing the Future

1. This time hear what is going on in the event you have just visualized.

Exercise 11–9: Investing the Future with Feelings

1. Now dwell on the feelings your character's expectations call up.

Exercise 11–10: Discovering Needs

1. After doing the dialogue two or three times, choose a need that seems consistent with the last three exercises.

2. Conclude by doing the scene two or three more times. Dedicate your attention to one another.

Working with Needs

Once you have identified a character's needs, you have still to give them a place in your own emotional life. The goal of the following exercises is to supply ways to invest a character's needs with your own personal energy. The exercises will also help you allow needs to foster and shape your contact with other actors.

Exercise 11–11: Needs Dialogue

1. Construct a dialogue with your partner, using one of the needs you discovered in the last group of exercises. For example,

   A: "I need your support."

   B: "I need your attention."

2. Continue the dialogue for a minute by repeating your statement to one another.

3. Then begin moving *randomly* in relation to one another as you speak. Keep the movement continuous and vary its size and intensity as much as possible.

4. Continue the exercise for three or four minutes.

Guidelines: Recall that movement is a way of helping your chosen needs get into your body and impart an emotional charge. By adjusting your own movement to someone else's, you help your emotional energy to sponsor a reaching out rather than a turning in.

Exercise 11–12: Giving Needs a Specific Physical Shape

1. Stand facing one another.

2. Begin this exercise the same way you began the last one.

3. As you do the "needs dialogue," try to find a simple physical movement or large gesture that captures and expresses the need. The more of your body you involve the better. For example, "I need attention" might give rise to a short burst of tap dancing. "I need a hug" might be physicalized by imitating the manner of a cuddly puppy.

4. Use your movement only on your own line and use it to communicate your need to your partner.

5. Continue the exercise until your choice of movement settles and becomes fluid and easy.

6. Gradually reduce the size of your physical work until it clings to the dialogue only as a residue. This process of gradual diminution will take place more easily if you remember to focus your attention on your partner. As your partner reduces the size of his or her work, so will you.

Exercise 11–13: Back to the Text

1. Now, restore the text on which your need statement is based.

2. Do the dialogue two or three times, allowing the physical residue you developed in the last exercise to become part of the interaction with your partner.

Exercise 11–14: Need Association

1. Make an associative grid for the need you identified in the last exercise. This can be done simply by writing or saying words and short phrases evoked by the need you are working with.

2. The associations can be purely imaginary or remembered. For example,
   Need Statement: "I need greater security."
   Associative Grid: my mother turning on the lights in a dark room, chocolate, pasta, leaning my back against someone I like and trust, a warm sleeping bag on a cold night

3. You might want to do this exercise privately first, then with your partner, trading associations back and forth in a dialogue.

Guidelines: Like the previous two exercises, this one can bring on considerable involvement in the needs of your character. To get as much as possible out of the exercise, you must be courageous and honest.

Exercise 11–15: Back to the Text

1. Play the dialogue you have been using.

2. Invite the effects of the previous dialogue to remain by using the same partner with whom you traded associations.

REFERENCES

Maslow, Abraham. *Motivation and Personality.* New York: Harper and Row, 1974. Although first published in 1954, this book is still a classic in the field of motivation. There is a great deal in it on which interested students might want to meditate.

(Notes, ideas, sketches, reactions to the exercises . . .)

*(Notes, ideas,
sketches, reactions
to the exercises . . .)*

*(Notes, ideas,
sketches, reactions
to the exercises . . .)*

_____

_____

_____

_____

_____

_____

_____

_____

_____

_____

_____

_____

_____

_____

_____

_____

_____

Obstacles and Stakes:

The Intensifiers of Action

OBSTACLES

An obstacle is anything that challenges or stands in the way of a character's intention. For example, if your intention is to insult someone who is hard of hearing, the character's crusty eardrums are an obstacle. To complete your intention, you must choose a means that will overcome the obstacle. For instance, to get your insult through to someone with bad hearing, you might have to yell. Your entire action, then, might be:

> intention: to insult
>
> means: by shouting

The important point is that the means of an intention must be capable of defeating whatever obstacle stands in the way of what your character is trying to do.

Not all obstacles are physical. Some may be psychological and take the form of a character's internal anxieties and inhibitions. For example, in her scene with the Gentleman Caller, Laura's obstacles might include the anxiety she feels over being alone with a man for the first time, or her fear of being found unattractive, or both. Other obstacles are social, such as norms that prohibit certain kinds of behavior. In *King Lear,* the great norm that makes Cordelia's first conversation with her father so difficult is "honor thy father," which Lear has translated into: "Children should do

Obstacle. Latin: impedimentum, . . . a hindrance, . . . baggage. Latin: impedire, to entangle, ensnare, . . . to render impassable.

Stake. Latin: pignus, a pledge, . . . secur- ity, . . . assurance, proof.

D. P. SIMPSON,
CASSELL'S NEW LATIN DICTIONARY

what they are told." To maintain her own integrity (and to more truly honor her father), Cordelia must resist his self-serving translation of the Fourth Commandment. While her responses are simple and brief, they are filled with the energy of one who is at war with an entire world order imposed upon her by a man with a distorted sense of himself. But no matter how internal or political their obstacles may be, the actors playing Laura and Cordelia must find means that are physical. Otherwise, their attempts to achieve their scene objectives will remain invisible to an audience.

Not all obstacles have the same impact on a character. The more powerful the obstacle, the more energy is demanded to overcome it. *The power of an obstacle helps to regulate the intensity with which actors play their actions.* It usually requires more effort to sell a car to a person fraught with suspicion than to one who is eager to buy.

Challenging roles require the actor to shift energy levels often, according to the differing magnitudes of the obstacles that impede the character's actions. Many of Shakespeare's most interesting characters are beset by a field of incessantly changing obstacles. The measure of these characters lies not only in their power to identify and address different obstacles but also in their ability to press their actions at the appropriate level of intensity. It is all too easy to overplay or underplay many of Shakespeare's characters. Juliet, for example, must contend with a headstrong and single-minded lover who is also a bit stupid, a good-hearted but inept nurse, a senseless family feud, a betrothal she does not want, and social norms that deprive a young woman of the freedom to determine her own destiny. The actress playing Juliet must always play at the "right size" proportional to the magnitude of the challenges that confront her. If the actress underplays an obstacle, she comes off weak or simpering. If she overplays, she comes off strident and whining.

OBSTACLES AND CONFLICT

Conflict is germane to most forms of drama. For actors, obstacles provide the conflict that shapes the energy and creates the emotional climate in each beat of a play. Obstacles are really opposing forces against which a character must strive in order to have his or her way.

As Robert Cohen has noted, on stage as in sports, winning is the primary goal. Not all characters win in every scene. Sometimes the obstacles prevail. But the actor's obligation is usually to make the character put up a good fight.

To act effectively, you must realize when your character wins and loses. Taking the time to enjoy victories and suffer defeats will help you to dimensionalize a character and increase his or her emotional diversity.

EXERCISES: OBSTACLES

Embodying Obstacles Through Conflict

The purpose of this first set of exercises is to help you grasp the relationship between obstacles and conflict. They provide a good warm-up for the rest of the chapter.

Exercise 12–1: Hand-to-Hand Combat

1. Stand in the middle of the acting space with a partner.
2. Press the palms and fingers of both hands against those of your partner.
3. Now start pushing. Try to push one another off balance.
4. As you push against one another, one of you say "yes," the other "no." Repeat the dialogue until the contest is over.

Exercise 12–2: Tag

1. Play tag with your partner.
2. During the chase, the one who is "it" should say "yes," the other "no."

Exercise 12–3: Arm Wrestling

1. Arm wrestle with your partner.
2. Incorporate the following dialogue into your work:
   A: "Please stay."
   B: "No, I must go."

Exercise 12–4: Apple Chasing

1. Dangle an apple on a string while your partner tries to take a bite out of it with his or her hands clasped behind the back.
2. Make your partner's task difficult but not impossible.
3. During the exercise, use the following exchange:
   A: "I want it."
   B: "You can't have it."
4. Now, trade roles and repeat the exercise.

Exercise 12–5: Paper Tag

1. Wad up some scratch paper and have a paper fight with your partner. For the sake of safety, aim for the legs only.

2. The one who scores the most hits wins.

3. As you play, add the "yes-no" dialogue.

Guidelines: Be careful. Even paper can put eyes and ears at risk.

Exercise 12–6: Incorporating a Dramatic Text

1. Now memorize a short text (or use one you already know).

2. Repeat each of the exercises you have just done using the new dialogue.

Obstacles from the Given Circumstances

Characters are often at odds with some part of the fictive world in which they live. Consequently, the given circumstances that make up that world generally provide a number of obstacles that may be used in a particular scene. The next exercises will help you discover and use obstacles from the environments, agents, events, and time constraints that make up dramatic situations.

Exercise 12–7: Obstacles and the Stage Environment

1. Pretend you and your partner are typists in a small office. *Your work stations are located near one another but not quite close enough to see the other's computer screen clearly.*

2. Both of you are trying to read what the other is typing.

3. There is no need for dialogue. Just experiment with various ways of overcoming the obstacle.

Exercise 12–8: Applications to the Text

1. Examine the dialogue you have memorized for this chapter.

2. Together with your partner, decide on an environment that seems to fit the text. (If you were working in a full-scale production, much of the environment would be indicated by the designer and director. But for now, it is best to use your imagination as well as your own sense of what the text is about.)

3. Then discover what obstacles the environment might offer you. Remember that finding obstacles is usually easier *after* you have decided on your character's intentions (infinitives).

4. Now play the scene two or three times using the spatial obstacles you have chosen. As you work, you may want to make changes in the intentions and/or obstacles you have chosen.

Exercise 12–9: Obstacles from Agents

1. Once again, use the dialogue you have memorized.

2. Review your scene objectives. Change them if you wish. Listen to the text carefully to discover an obstacle that is associated with the other character. For example, maybe the other character is overbearing, or stubborn, or mean, or angry, or too in love or full of hate to listen to you. Focus on personality traits.

3. Now, rehearse your dialogue. As you do so, find something in your partner's appearance or behavior that makes the obstacle real. There might be something about the set of her jaw, her tone of voice, or the way she smiles or gestures that seems contrary or opposed to what you are trying to do or get.

4. Now play the dialogue again, concentrating on the obstacle you have found in the last step.

5. Take this exercise one step further by trying to find a physical or vocal means to override or somehow cancel out the physical obstacle you have found in your partner. For example, if her smirk catches your attention, perhaps a smile on your part will overcome it; if her feet seem planted solidly against you, perhaps shouting will gain you the upper hand; and so on.

Exercise 12–10: Obstacles and Events

1. Review the paradigm for finding an event provided in Chapter 7.

2. Run through your dialogue and choose the event that you believe is happening to your character. For example, "This job is killing me"; or, "She [or he] is hurting me."

3. Then answer the following question: "What about the event makes it harder to accomplish my intention?" The answer is the obstacle presented by the event. Keep the wording as simple as possible.

4. Now play the dialogue, attempting to overcome the obstacle you have identified.

Exercise 12–11: Obstacles and Time

Preliminary note: Lack of time is a frequent obstacle in much Western drama. For example, in Georges Feydeau's *Hotel Paradiso*, the pathologically nervous Mr. Pettibone escapes to a sleazy hotel with his next door neighbor's wife. They have decided to have an affair but have only a short time to complete their plans. What is more, each is utterly terrified. In Neil Simon's *Plaza Suite,* Roy's daughter, Mimsey, locks herself in the bathroom before her wedding and refuses to budge. Roy must race the clock to get his daughter out before the guests discover there is something wrong.

1. Run through your dialogue once or twice.

2. Review your scene objectives.

3. Now do your scene or jump three times. Each time reduce the amount of time you have to accomplish your action.

Guidelines: It's not just a matter of getting through your lines faster. Anyone can hurry. The acting problem is to remain dedicated to your action (i.e., to pursue your objective thoroughly), in spite of the pressures of time. In other words, don't let "to hurry" take the place of your real intention. Simply try to accomplish it more quickly with each repetition. This might mean changing the means to your intention in order to press it home more rapidly.

Substitutions

Playing obstacles successfully often requires a technique called "substitution." Substitution involves finding *personal images or concrete physical analogies* that capture the obstacle you are working with. The purpose is to help the obstacle affect you deeply and evoke responses appropriate to the script.

Exercise 12–12: Private Secrets Out Loud

1. Play the following improvisation: Your partner is a policeman who is interrogating you for a crime you did not commit.

2. Feelings of fear and embarrassment are your obstacles.

3. Substitution: Imagine that each question is really a loud, public announcement of a very private secret, things you have never told anyone.

Exercise 12–13: The Pub

1. You and your partner are in a pub trying to clarify a class assignment that neither of you quite understood.

2. The obstacle is the loud band that makes hearing difficult.

3. Substitution: Put cotton in your ears before you begin the scene.

Exercise 12–14: The Sales Shield

1. Your partner is trying to persuade you to buy a used car.
2. Pretend his or her words are arrows.
3. Use a shield to protect yourself from his or her persuasion.

Guidelines: Notice that this exercise makes use of both an image (arrows) and a concrete physical analogy (a shield).

Exercise 12–15: Back to the Text

1. Examine the dialogue you have memorized.
2. Choose an obstacle.
3. Use an image and/or a physical analogy to make the obstacle concrete for yourself. Then repeat the dialogue several times.
4. As you do so, shift your concentration from your image or analogy to your partner. If the effect of the exercise does not cling to your work, go back to step 3 for a while.

STAKES

Stakes are what your character stands to win or lose in a particular situation. They are like rewards and punishments. For example, during the balcony scene, Romeo stands to win a glimpse of Juliet, but he also stands to lose his life. The risks are high, but he is a man smitten with a love that upends reason.

Stakes are intimately connected to obstacles and actions. A character wins stakes by overcoming obstacles and accomplishing an action. Romeo's action might be to make contact with Juliet by hiding in her garden and climbing a tree (for a better view of her bedchamber). The obstacles are many and stem from the hostility between the families of the two lovers. The garden is enemy territory, and there is no telling when a band of Juliet's kinsmen might happen upon Romeo.

The actor playing Romeo must choose a specific *perspective* toward his stakes. He may play as though he is more likely to win or as though there is a distinct chance of losing. The first is a power-up perspective; the other is power-down. A power-up perspective might give Romeo an air of confidence and make him seem aloof from the danger; playing power-down could color his behavior with a degree of wild abandon. Like obstacles, stakes contribute to the emotional intensity of an actor's work. So it is important to maintain variety both in the stakes you choose and in your perspective toward them.

EXERCISES: STAKES

Understanding Stakes in Your Own Life

The purpose of the first two exercises is to help you understand stakes from the point of view of your own life.

Exercise 12–16: Personal Stakes

1. Try to discover what you commonly feel is at stake in one of your more important relationships:

   a. What do you stand to gain from the relationship?

   b. What do you stand to lose?

   c. Do you most often feel you are gaining or losing, or are both going on at the same time?

   d. How does answering these questions make you feel about the relationship?

Guidelines: This exercise is really a meditation about the stakes in your own life. It is best done in silence. You may want to write about it in your journal.

Exercise 12–17: Playing for Real Stakes

1. Choose a meal that you really like.

2. Now do the following while saying "yes" or "no" to one another:

   a. Arm wrestle.

   b. Join palms and try to push one another off balance.

   c. Stand on one foot and try to knock each other off balance using pillows.

3. The winner of each contest has to make the other person's favorite meal.

Exercise 12–18: Incorporating Your Text

1. Repeat the exercise. While you battle, exchange lines from a dialogue you memorized for one of the previous chapters.

Stakes and Appetites

Stakes become more concrete when they are strongly associated with our most basic appetites. Our desires for food, sex, wealth, personal comfort, glory, and power over others and what they own often provide stakes that are useful in the theatre. Taken to excess, these appetites are none other than the seven deadly sins. Ironically, most dramatic characters—even the more positive ones—display an overabundance of one or the other of these appetites. Often, the difference between a "good" character and a "bad" character is that the former's appetites and the means to satisfying them are portrayed as acceptable within the fictive world of the play. Shakespeare's Henry V is a good example of a character whose appetites are given legitimacy by the play. Henry satisfies his appetite for power over land and people by invading France and killing ten thousand human beings. Shakespeare allows him to justify his appetite by emphasizing the French violation of laws and treaties. Moreover, depending on the director's view of war and history, the justification for Henry's action offered in the play may appear perfectly acceptable or altogether hollow or even morally ambiguous.

Exercise 12–19: Fantasizing Stakes

1. Memorize a new scene or jump.
2. Choose stakes that fit the text and are also based on one of your five appetites. (The baser the better.)
3. Run the dialogue twice slowly. As you do, fantasize how it would feel to win your stakes.
4. Now do it two more times as you fantasize losing.

Guidelines: Dwell on your fantasies rather than on acting.

Exercise 12–20: Embodying Your Fantasy

1. Find some position, posture, or movement that makes the fantasy more vivid. For example, if what's at stake is your power over others, you might want to stand on a chair over your partner. If glory is your choice, exaggerate the stance of a sports hero or politician in a victory parade.
2. Run the dialogue once or twice.
3. As you begin the dialogue a third time, have your partner try to alter your chosen position or movement. (Please remember to be careful.)
4. Fight to keep it.
5. Now switch places with your partner.
6. Then do the dialogue, allowing only the residues of the exercise to cling. As usual this is best done by focusing your attention on one another.

REFERENCES

Cohen, Robert. *Acting Power.* Mountain View, CA: Mayfield Publishing Co., 1978. See, especially, his discussions of victories and winning.

Hagen, Uta [with Haskel Frankel]. *Respect for Acting.* New York: Macmillan, 1973. Her discussion of substitution is particularly helpful.

*(Notes, ideas,
sketches, reactions
to the exercises . . .)*

(Notes, ideas, sketches, reactions to the exercises . . .)

(Notes, ideas, sketches, reactions to the exercises . . .)

Character Transformations

Character transformations, the theme of Part IV, are the changes we make in our own customary behavior in order to create a character. These changes are not merely a matter of adding a limp here or an accent there, however. Character transformation is really a rich process of self-discovery, through which we find a different and perhaps unaccustomed side of ourselves that fits the character we are playing. As written in a script, the character is a kind of map that leads us to a particular version of ourselves that would otherwise remain unexpressed and invisible both to us and to others.

I like the word transformation *because it is so suggestive. It means that the actor's identity is something like a piece of music. To play a character, the actor takes the notes apart and reorders them to form a new song. An actor* re-creates *himself or herself in order to create a character.*

This double act of creation and re-creation is thoroughly social. The actor, transformed by the character, stimulates the audience to begin a process of self-transformation analogous to the actor's own. Audience members come to a deeper sense of their own identities and their own potential for personal change. Like a priest or shaman, the actor confronts others with the possibilities for growth and imbues them with the spiritual energy to continue growing after the play is over.

In many ways the actor is the closest thing to God. Because he has the privilege and honor to create another human being.
ROD STEIGER,
"COMMENTS ON ACTING"

"Acting like this is a dream," you say. But it is a dream worth working for. It is a matter of committing yourself to artistic values that make acting a gift to others instead of a self-centered demand for love and recognition.

Body Centers

Not all characters move in precisely the same way. They shape motion differently, depending, among other things, on which body centers they use to give form to their physical effort. *A body center is a physical location from which movement and position are initiated and organized.* Some characters seem to alter their body centers in response to different situations. Others cling to the same one no matter what. Flexibility varies.

In our own everyday lives, the preference of one body center over another may be a matter of upbringing and habit rather than conscious choice (issues discussed in Part I). But for actors on stage the opposite must become true. Centers must be chosen in accord with the character and then become habit.

Inasmuch as they influence the body in action, body centers inevitably have a major impact on the style of a character's communication, including vocal timbre and inflection. In the following exercises, you will be working with five centers of particular use in developing a character's body: the head, the upper torso (shoulders and upper chest), the midtorso (the area of the heart and diaphragm), the lower torso (abdomen and pelvis), and the knees. The way you and your character use these centers creates dynamic differences in how you move and position yourselves in the world. Exercises from Part I are a natural preparation for the work to come.

The first four exercise sequences will help you discover different ways of working with body centers. The fifth sequence applies what you have learned to characterization and text work.

One thing a person can never do is fool himself. There are many actors of great talent who have sold their artistic integrity. They drive Cadillacs and have fine homes. But why do they get drunk and cry at 2:00 A.M. and apologize for their work?

ROD STEIGER,
"COMMENTS ON ACTING"

EXERCISES

Playing with Body Centers

The exercises in this series work best when done playfully. It is important to remember that the work you do with your body has a psychological and emotional dimension. Working on a character's body helps to trigger his or her inner life as well.

Exercise 13–1: Moving from the Head

1. Start walking from the head. This is easily done by leaning your head in a particular direction and letting the rest of your body follow.
2. Change speed and direction frequently. Exaggerate.
3. Try different kinds of movement: sitting, standing, lying down, and so on.

Exercise 13–2: Continuations

1. Repeat the exercise once for each body center.

Exercise 13–3: Moving to Music

1. Play your favorite album of big band music.
2. Dance with various partners using different body centers for each dance.

Exercise 13–4: Center/Body Split

1. Pretend your head wants to move in one direction but the rest of your body prefers another, so that you are trying to move in two different directions at the same time.
2. Your head wins the contest, but the rest of your body follows reluctantly.

Exercise 13–5: Continuations

1. Repeat the exercise once for each center.

Guidelines: Remember you are pitting the "will" of only one center against the "will" of the rest of your body. Avoid separating yourself into too many pieces.

Exercise 13–6: Animal Inventions

1. Pick a body center.
2. Choose an animal that seems to move from that center.
3. Imitate the animal as closely as possible, paying particular attention to how it uses its center to organize movement.
4. Explore all the ways the animal moves. Move around the room, greeting other "animals" with whatever sounds you think your animal would make.
5. After five or six minutes, begin restoring yourself to your human form. But maintain the animal's body center in your own posture and movement.

Exercise 13–7: Variations

1. Explore other body centers using different animals.

Centers and the Impulse to Move

The next sequence will sensitize you to different kinds of impulses that induce movement. *In general, there are two kinds of impulses: voluntary and involuntary.* Voluntary impulses make your character's movement seem completely self-determined, as though it stems simply from the personal decision to move. Involuntary impulses, on the other hand, feel completely or partially directed by psychological or social forces outside your character's control. *Involuntary impulses shape movement as though a character were being pushed or pulled.* It will be easier to talk about the various kinds of impulses after you have done a few of the exercises.

Exercise 13–8: Cycle I: Voluntary
Movement from the Head

1. First, develop a flexible and light feeling in the head and neck by doing some gentle head rotations. (Stop before you get dizzy.)
2. Now let your head lead the rest of your body around the room.
3. Experiment with changes in direction and speed.
4. Stay tuned to the sensations in your body. How does your movement feel?

Exercise 13–9: Cycle II: Pulling Movement from the Head

1. Now pretend there is a string attached to some part of your head (e.g., your nose, chin, tongue) and that you are being pulled around the room.

2. Explore variations by changing the *force* of the pull, its *direction,* and its *attitude* (i.e., friendly, harsh, angry, happy, sad, or whatever). Work with one attitude at a time.

Exercise 13–10: Cycle III: Pushing Movement into the Head

1. Pretend that some outside force is pushing your head first in one direction, then in another. The rest of your body follows your head around the room.

2. Again, vary the force, direction, and attitude of the push.

Exercise 13–11: Upper Torso I, II, III

1. Before beginning, warm up by doing large shoulder rotations. Do one shoulder at a time, then both together. Keep the movement light and easy.

2. Apply the last three exercises to the shoulders and upper chest. First, let the impulse for your movement be *self-initiated.* Then let it come as the result of a *pull,* then from a *push.*

3. Remember, you can originate movement from each of your shoulders separately, or both together. Experiment.

Exercise 13–12: Midtorso I, II, III

1. Warm up by placing your hands on your hips and making large circles with your whole torso. Again, do not press. Keep the work light and gentle.

2. Now do the cycle of three exercises you have been using. Work with your heart region, midback, and so on.

Exercise 13–13: Lower Torso I, II, III

1. Warm up by doing hip circles.

2. Repeat the same cycle of three exercises, this time focusing on the pelvis and lower abdomen.

Exercise 13–14: Moving from the Knees I, II, III

1. Warm up by doing large knee circles.

Body Centers, Movement Impulse, and Feeling

The next exercise and its variations give you the opportunity to explore the relationship among body centers, movement, and feelings.

Exercise 13–15: Emotional Statement

1. Repeat the three exercise cycles for each of the five body centers.

2. As you do so, try to find a simple statement that captures your emotional reaction. For example, while exploring what it feels like to be pulled by the head, you might say, "I hate being pulled around the room like this." If working with push impulses in the midtorso, you might come upon the phrase, "Quit shoving my heart around." Some of your phrases might be even simpler: "I feel so free" or "This is fun." The important thing is to be honest. If you don't want to make your feelings public, just say "no" or "yes," depending on whether you like how your movement feels.

3. Let each exercise create your vocal quality. Just breathe freely and let your voice go.

The three sets of exercises you have completed so far apply the notions of voluntary and involuntary movement (i.e., pushing and pulling) to the task of shaping a character's body and motion. Cycle I exercises give you the opportunity to experiment with how it feels to move voluntarily from various centers. But many complex characters often seem moved by outside forces that pull (cycle II) and push (cycle III) them. Part of their struggle is to reclaim their bodies and wills. For example, according to some interpretations, Macbeth is a man who is pushed and pulled through the first two-thirds of his play. But in the last stage of his career, Macbeth changes. His body and movement become more his own as he comes to will his own destiny. In *Bus Stop,* Dr. Lyman is pushed and pulled by the booze he carries with him. Regardless of his intentions, he is always within its gravitational force. Unlike Macbeth, he never successfully takes charge of himself.

Approaching Character

These next exercises are meant to accomplish two purposes: (1) to help you apply what you have learned about body centers and movement impulses directly to characterization, and (2) to develop a theme that so far has been only implicit. *That is, the pushes and pulls that shape the way a character uses his or her centers may seem to originate either in the external world or within the character.* "Seem" is an important word for I am really talking about how impulse feels, its sensuous quality. Guilt, greed, fear, hope, love, duty, lust, and so on make great internal pushers and pullers, whereas food, booze, money, and sexy others may seem to exert external pressure. When the pushes and pulls are extreme, they become compulsions.

The exercises begin with voluntary impulses as a point of departure. That way involuntary impulses can be more vivid. As you move through the exercises, notice the differing sensations and feelings created by both voluntary and involuntary impulses.

Exercise 13–16: Voluntary Impulse

Situation notes: Your character works in a restaurant. Your job is to clean off tables. You notice a dirty cup.

1. Movement pattern: Cross to the table and clear off the cup. Your movement is self-directed, originating with the simple decision to clean the table.

2. Experiment with moving from each of the five body centers.

Guidelines: A self-directed person is often better aligned than one whose body is pushed and pulled. But self-directed movement is not always fun or pleasant. Cleaning tables might be boring.

Exercise 13–17: Involuntary Movement: External Pushing and Pulling

Situation notes: You are an alcoholic sitting in a bar. You have no money but are obsessed with getting something to drink. You see a half-full glass of wine at an empty table.

1. Movement pattern 1: Pretend the glass is pulling you toward it. You resist, but it eventually wins. Cross to the glass as if being pulled by the head (i.e., the lips, tongue, or throat). Make the attitude of the impulse clear.

2. Movement pattern 2: Repeat the cross, this time as though being pushed from behind your head by an evil demon.

3. Experiment with feeling pushes and pulls in other body centers. Remember to resist the impulse at first, then let it overcome you.

Guidelines: Experiment with different sizes of impulse and movement. The broader your physical work, the more cartoonlike the character is apt to become. Playing your transformations at a more subtle level can create a more naturalistic character.

Exercise 13–18: Pushed and Pulled by an Internal State

Situation notes: You are standing outside a hospital room. The person in the bed was badly injured due to your negligence. You have come to apologize.

1. Movement pattern 1: In spite of your fear and embarrassment, you feel pushed toward the hospital room by your own sense of guilt. Try to feel the pushing on your back, behind your heart. Next, let the guilt attack your knees and start them walking into the room. Repeat this step using other centers.
2. Movement pattern 2: Now you feel pulled toward the room by the presence of the person in the hospital bed. Begin experimenting by feeling the tug in the midtorso, your heart. Then work with other centers.
3. Remember, entering the room is not easy. Let the pushing and pulling overcome your resistance gradually. Also, clarify the attitude of the impulses.

Exercise 13–19: From External to Internal Impulses

1. Clean off the cup again.
2. Movement pattern 1: This time your boss is watching. His or her presence pushes you to the cup. (external)
3. Movement pattern 2: This is the last job you have to complete before going home. So, the cup is your ticket to freedom. Let it pull you to the table. (external)
4. Movement pattern 3: This time a sense of responsibility pushes or pulls (choose the one that fits best with your concept of responsibility) you to the table. (internal)

Exercise 13–20: Working from a Text

1. Choose a dialogue and memorize it.
2. Run lines with your partner a few times.
3. Now answer the following questions:
   a. From what center does your character's movement originate?
   b. What kind of impulse makes the center move: Voluntary or involuntary? External? Internal?
   c. What is the attitude of the impulse?

Guidelines: A short text (or even a long one for that matter) cannot supply all the answers. Use your imagination and do not be afraid to make inferences.

Exercise 13–21: Using Your Answers I

1. Walk around the room in a big circle.
2. Explore ways of using the center you chose when you answered the questions in the previous exercise until you discover one that fits your character.
3. Now do the dialogue with your partner while you are both moving around the room. Exaggerate your movement sometimes.
4. Let your movement pattern change your voice.

Exercise 13–22: Using Your Answers II

1. Now use the type of impulse you selected when you answered the questions.
2. Experiment freely with different ways of moving from the impulse you have chosen. Remember the impulse can be intense or subtle. It can also have an attitude.

Exercise 13–23: Synthesis I

1. Put together the choices you made in the last two exercises (a particular center + a particular impulse). Move randomly for three or four minutes while trading lines with your partner.
2. Try your movement pattern at various sizes and levels of intensity.
3. Notice what happens to your voice.
4. Do the dialogue while sitting or standing relatively still. Use an alignment that results directly from your movement pattern.

Exercise 13–24: Synthesis II

1. Choose a simple piece of business with your partner. You can tie your shoes, comb your hair, arrange light furniture, stack books, mop the floor, drink coffee—anything that fits your text.
2. Perform the business using the centers and impulses from the last exercise.
3. After a minute or two, incorporate your dialogue.

Exercise 13–25: Integration

1. After class, find a friend to talk to.
2. During the conversation, use the kinesthetic organization you have just been working with. See if you can maintain your new body pattern without distracting the other person from the conversation.
3. The goal is to integrate the changes you made for your scene and use them as natural parts of your communication.

Exercise 13–26: Circling Back

1. Do the scene or jump again.
2. At this point, your physical changes have probably begun to feel more natural and easier to maintain. If not, go back through the last five exercises. Take your time.

REFERENCES

Klein, Maxine. *Time, Space, and Designs for the Actor.* Boston: Houghton Mifflin Company, 1975. For an alternate view of body centers, the student may want to take a look at Chapter 4. Klein enumerates four centers: mind, heart, stomach, and genitals.

Penrod, James. *Movement for the Performing Artist.* Mountain View: Mayfield Publishing, 1974. The author includes exercises on what he refers to as energy centers on page 7.

*(Notes, ideas,
sketches, reactions
to the exercises . . .)*

---

*(Notes, ideas,
sketches, reactions
to the exercises . . .)*

_____

_____

_____

_____

_____

_____

_____

_____

_____

_____

_____

_____

_____

_____

_____

_____

_____

_____

*(Notes, ideas,
sketches, reactions
to the exercises . . .)*

_____

_____

_____

_____

_____

_____

_____

_____

_____

_____

_____

_____

_____

_____

_____

_____

_____

Body Strategies: Rigid, Dense, Collapsed, Swollen

Body strategies are the specific shapes we take on in order to pursue actions and overcome obstacles in our everyday lives. For example, we shape ourselves one way to get a raise from a boss we seldom see and scarcely know, and another way to ask a neighbor to take in our mail for a couple of days. Body strategies are psychophysical. Different physical shapes also incorporate personal feelings, social attitudes, and cognitive patterns—a sense of fear or confidence, warmth or aloofness, an inkling of what and how much to say. Body strategies, then, are really ways we deploy and use ourselves to carry on a rewarding exchange with the physical and social environment.

In *Emotional Anatomy,* Stanley Keleman outlines four major body strategies. He calls them *rigid, dense, collapsed, and swollen.* Each of these terms describes a body strategy that has been taken to the extreme. But few people, if any, fit these extremes. Most people are very specific combinations of all four. Moreover, an ideally healthy person can take on those qualities from each type that are most advantageous in a particular situation. Of course, not all people are ideally healthy. Some have suffered a reduction in their capacity to shape themselves advantageously. They get stuck in ruts and lose their ability to adapt to particular situations.

The same is true of dramatic characters. In fact, the practicality of describing extreme types stems, in part, from the fact that most interesting characters are "mis-shapen," at least to some degree. That is, their particular blend of body strategies is in some sense skewed or out of balance. These dramatic characters are literally at odds with themselves because, in spite of their efforts, they shape themselves in ways that are not quite in

[Bodily] shape . . . represents how we view the world and try to interact with it. . . . We relate to others via the [somatic] forms we make. . . .
STANLEY KELEMAN,
EMOTIONAL ANATOMY

sync with what they want or need from the dramatic world. On stage, characters who learn are often those who discover how to reshape themselves to achieve their actions.

THE RIGID STRUCTURE

Taken to the extreme, the rigid strategy has the following characteristics: The head is held erect and level by means of neck muscles that are always somewhat tensed to keep the head in position. Rigid personalities suck in their lower torso. This forces breathing into the chest, creating a V-shaped physique with overdeveloped shoulders and a flared chest. Overall vocal quality is full but forced because of the energy needed to overcome the inhibition from the contracted neck and expanded chest. The upper torso is kept erect and rigid by tightening the buttocks and thighs and locking the knees.

The rigid person thinks of himself as a doer. His core statements might be: "Step aside"; "I'm stronger than you are"; "I can do it"; "I'll save you"; "I'm in charge"; or "Follow me." These attitudes may work positively or negatively, depending on the situation. Rigid personalities relate to others by challenge, competition, or active service. They are good at establishing strong personal boundaries and like to push against obstacles rather than circumvent them in some way. Self-control, discipline, duty, loyalty, and strength are primary values. Rigid persons often have a clear and simple sense of right and wrong. Ambiguity and inconclusiveness make them uncomfortable. They prefer the roles of leader, boss, hero, or crusader.

Because his body is overly braced, the rigid type has trouble becoming aware of softer feelings, which he associates with weakness. He specializes in anger, which is easier to access through contracted muscles.

The rigid type wins at tug-of-war by preparing his team carefully and leading by example. The rigid typology is *part* of the basis for several generations of American male heroes: John Wayne, Sylvester Stallone, Alan Ladd, Arnold Schwarzenegger, Chuck Norris, and sometimes Henry Fonda and Robert Redford. Many contemporary advertisements for health clubs and gyms present an intensely muscled young person who is the very image of extreme rigidity.

THE DENSE STRUCTURE

The dense body shape is compacted and held in, something like a water balloon that has been squeezed at both ends. A cartoonist might make a dense character look like a bulldog or human fireplug. Her shoulders are held high and blend into the neck, which seems short and muscular. The upper back and shoulders are usually rounded forward as though bearing weight from above. She is durable and can take on a lot. Head and upper torso tend to lack flexibility, and function as a single unit. Instead of being sucked in, like her rigid counterpart's, her stomach is more apparent because the muscles are chronically contracted. Thighs and buttocks are disproportionately thick to help balance the large, frozen mass that sits on top of them. Her voice has a knot in it as though she were talking while carrying a trunk up a flight of stairs.

"Make me"; "I dare you"; "Lean on me"; "I'll carry you"; and "Don't humiliate me" are core statements that give meaning to the dense type's way of standing in the world. Part of the strategy behind the physical structure is to maintain close contact with others but without letting them affect her too deeply or allowing them to see her feelings. Feelings are dangerous for a person with a dense structure because they almost always seem to come up without warning. One of her greatest fears is that her feelings will go out of control and cause personal humiliation. So, she prefers emotional restraint to the risk of explosion.

The dense personality is stubborn rather than challenging, resistant rather than competitive, and can be very supportive. While she may not be overtly nurturing, she is good at giving people room to do what they wish. She is capable of appearing cool and can stabilize a group as well as provide good advice and encouragement. Other core statements might be: "Go ahead and try it"; "Let's work this out together." Underneath it all, the dense type is full of passion just waiting for a chance to get out. Sometimes it does, usually as an eruption.

Dense personalities often play roles that require resistance, long-term struggle, perseverance, and analytic intelligence. She wins at tug-of-war partially by careful planning, partially by compensating for weaker team members, and partially by digging in her heels and waiting for the other team to wear out.

THE COLLAPSED STRUCTURE

The chest muscles of the collapsed body strategy are much looser than those of the rigid type. In extreme cases, the entire chest cavity is concave, which produces a rounded back and positions the neck at a forward angle with the head placed nearly over the stomach. Lower torso and hips protrude forward so that the rear end rolls under. To keep his feet flat on the floor, the collapsed person must bend at the knees. Again, these characteristics can vary in degree.

Statements that get to the core of this type's personality might be: "I can't"; "I give up"; "Rescue me"; "Hold me up"; "Anything you say"; or

"Yes." The collapsed morphology produces easy access to feelings of despair, resignation, and submission. The world is too heavy and too painful. Unlike his dense counterpart who struggles against the weight, the collapsed type lets himself be crushed or molded entirely by outside pressure.

People with collapsed tendencies are better than rigid or dense persons at letting go of relationships or tasks that are not working. Moreover, their passivity makes for some degree of adaptability. They are able to give the support they themselves need and are often humble and unobtrusive.

Collapsed personalities can experience hostility quite vividly, but they vent aggression by making others feel guilty for victimizing them. Although they prefer to have others take responsibility for virtually everything, they also feel imposed upon by the choices others make.

Collapsed individuals "win" at tug-of-war by letting go of the rope.

THE SWOLLEN STRUCTURE

The swollen morphology is pear-shaped with an expanded stomach. Relative to the lower torso, the shoulders and chest appear squeezed and narrow. This shape is not due to overweight but to the way the muscles are organized and held. The stance is usually slightly wide, with the feet at or just outside the shoulder line. But there is little sense of solidity. The swollen personality is often unsure of her ground and has trouble feeling planted or stable.

Statements that summarize the swollen person's fundamental attitudes might include: "You need me"; "Take me into your world"; "Let me get to you"; "Give me structure"; "Hug me and let me hug you." She deals with obstacles by expanding against them. She can be manipulative, possessive, and invasive. The personal boundaries of others may mean little to her. She feels everyone needs her special touch, whether they know it or not.

At her best, the swollen type is a good listener, nurturing and empathic. As part of her support, she is willing to play whatever roles others require of her as long as her efforts are appreciated. She includes people in her life even as she wishes to be included in theirs.

She wins at tug-of-war by throwing a party for the other team.

USING THE TYPOLOGIES

The four body strategies just described can provide a starting point for some provocative character work. Here are a few guidelines to keep in mind while you are doing the exercises.

1. Playing an extreme version of any of the four types usually leads to a presentational, comic character of the sort you might see in a Saturday morning cartoon, a vaudeville sketch, or a slapstick farce.

2. Where naturalism or less exaggerated styles of acting are required, the typologies can be seen as scenarios for exploration rather than formulae for final results. In other words, instead of presenting one of the types at full force, you will probably use only subtle *residues* of the muscular adjustments you have acquired through the exercises.

3. In many cases, it is best to use just a few traits from one or more body strategies in order to achieve an effective character shape. Subtle characterization is sometimes best.

4. Because each typology is really a strategy for dealing with events as they develop, you may want to make adjustments, depending on the situation your character is in. For example, you might give Juliet *some* of the character structure of the rigid type when she puts off Paris in IV.i; then let her collapse a little (or a lot) after the Friar closes the door to the confessional. ("O shut the door! and when thou hast done so,/Come weep with me—past hope, past cure, past help.") One of the most important questions you can ask is: "When and how does my character change?" Too many major changes and the character seems hyperkinetic, too few and he or she becomes one-dimensional and impervious to incoming stimuli.

5. Recall that each typology is not a mere disguise but a path to self-transformation, which implies inward as well as outward change.

6. Most often, it is best to play your character's body strategies as positively as possible. Characters usually do not know when they are "misshaping" themselves in a way that is detrimental or in some sense ineffective. In many cases, your job will be to compose a body shape and make it appealing.

Emotion is behavior. Anger, rage, fear, terror, pleasure, joy—all have a clear muscular and visceral shape. . . .

STANLEY KELEMAN,
EMOTIONAL ANATOMY

EXERCISES

Embodying Each Typology

The purpose of the first series of exercises is to help you become acquainted with each of the character shapes just discussed.

Exercise 14–1: Exploring a Different Shape

1. Choose one of the types and read the description slowly.

2. Visualize yourself as that type without actually making any of the adjustments. Take your time and notice where the new image of yourself is clear and where it is not. Perhaps you will have an easy time visualizing a new head position but a more difficult time imagining the position of your hips.

3. Now, begin making the appropriate physical adjustments, starting with those that were clearest to you. Exaggerate.

4. When you feel you have achieved the bodily shape you've chosen, perform the following experiments:
   a. Practice sitting and standing.
   b. Take a walk around the room in your new form.
   c. Vocalize by repeating a line or two from something you've already memorized. Let your body shape determine the sound.

Exercise 14–2: Continuation

1. Repeat the exercise, exploring each of the typologies in the same way.
2. Take your time.

Exercise 14–3: Inner Life

1. Choose a body type.
2. Move into it gradually.
3. Exaggerate the shape until it becomes a little uncomfortable.
4. Locate the muscle groups that are uncomfortable.
5. Gradually loosen your muscles, allowing yourself to come back to your own normal shape.
6. As you loosen, report your inner life (feelings, associations, memories, desires) out loud to your partner or the class. If something embarrassing comes up, say "pass" and go on to your next awareness.

Exercise 14–4: Continuation

1. Repeat the last exercise once for each body shape.

Exploring Attitudes

Somatic forms also embody larger social attitudes, which are part of the basis for your relationship with others. The next few exercises will help you explore some of the attitudes that become available with Keleman's four body types.

Exercise 14–5: Core Statements

1. Review the core statements associated with each typology.

    Rigid: "I'm in charge"; "Follow me"; "I'm a winner"; "I'm stronger than you are"; "I can do it"; "I'll save you."

    Dense: "Make me"; "I dare you"; "Give it a try"; "Let's work on this together."

    Collapsed: "I give up"; "At your service"; "Use me"; "Save me"; "Hold me up."

    Swollen: "Choose me"; "Let me get under your skin"; "Hug me and let me hug you"; "Give me more room."

2. Choose a body structure. Exaggerate a bit but keep it comfortable. Stand in front of the class and say each of the core statements that match your shape.

3. Starting with the first statement, repeat each three or four times. While you do so, refine your physical shape by making small adjustments until your statement feels natural and honest.

Exercise 14–6: Continuation

1. Repeat the exercise once for each body type.

Exercise 14–7: Core Dialogue

1. You and your partner choose different body types.
2. Repeat the appropriate core statements to one another as a dialogue.

Blending and Modulating Body Shapes

Now that you've had some time to explore each shape and some of its emotional and social associations, it is time to work with traits from more than one typology and to use them at different levels of intensity.

Exercise 14–8: Opposite Combinations

1. Choose one adjustment from an overbound form (rigid or dense) and one from an underbound form (collapsed or swollen). For example, you might select the flared chest of the rigid type and the bent knees of the collapsed type.

2. Shuttle back and forth from one to the next. Quicken the rhythm gradually into an upbeat motion.

3. Slow down gradually. Eventually find a balance between the two traits and stand still.

4. Experiment with your new shape by sitting, standing, and walking. Make your changes comfortable and as pleasant as possible.

Exercise 14–9: Finding the Dominant Feelings

1. Continue moving around the room.

2. As you meet other classmates, exchange a dialogue in which you each make a brief statement about how the physical transformation makes you feel. For example,

A: I'm angry.

B: I feel embarrassed.

C: I feel strong.

Your feelings may change from one encounter to the next.

Exercise 14–10: Discovering Social Attitudes

1. Continue your walk.

2. Discover a core statement that summarizes your attitude toward others and share it with those you meet, as in the last exercise.

3. Be sure to listen to what others say to you. For example,

A: I'm better than you.

B: Tell me what to do.

C: You are all better than me.

Working with a Text

Exercise 14–11: Word Work

1. Choose a dialogue and memorize it. A short scene is best here.

2. Run lines with your partner three or four times.

3. Underline an important verb in each of your character's sentences, then underline the important noun, then the adjective. (Verbs are usually the most active words in a sentence, with nouns and adjectives supplying sense and color.)

4. See if you can combine any of the words you underlined (regardless of where they occur) into a statement of social attitude or personal feeling. Fill in gaps with your own words as necessary. For example, "I have always traveled [with] machetes." (Mary in scene 2, *On the Verge*. These words have been chosen from a variety of Mary's lines.)

5. With the first four steps as preparation, select adjustments that seem to fit your character. Choose only a few traits from one or more body strategies.

6. Make the alterations comfortable by doing some normal movement, such as walking, tying your shoes, drinking a glass of water.

7. Now do the scene with your partner, concentrating on one another and letting go of your physical work.

Exercise 14–12: Beginning a Synthesis

Note: Remember that body strategies may be frozen character habits and/or they may be changeable ways of coping or reacting to given circumstances and obstacles.

1. Search through the scene for your character's given circumstances.

2. Discuss how they might refine or even suggest changes for your overall physical shape.

3. Make the alterations and do the scene a couple of times.

Exercise 14–13: Continuing the Synthesis I

1. Choose an action for your character.

2. Discuss which physical traits might help you achieve it.

3. Explore your choices by doing the scene several times. Be sure to use your adjustments as means.

Exercise 14–14: Continuing the Synthesis II

1. While certain physical traits might help you achieve actions, others may present obstacles.

2. Find these *if there are any.*

3. Use these obstacles to raise the intensity of your work as you repeat the scene again.

REFERENCES

Keleman, Stanley. *Embodying Experience.* Berkeley, CA: Center Press, 1987. The author applies his theory of human personality to a discussion of psychoemotional health and illness.

———. *Emotional Anatomy.* Berkeley, CA: Center Press, 1985. Cited earlier, this volume presents the rationale and descriptions of the four body strategies used in this chapter.

————. *Patterns of Distress.* Berkeley, CA: Center Press, 1989. This book continues the work of *Embodying Experience.*

Part of the value of Keleman's ideas is that they underscore the central role of the body in all aspects of acting. His approach does not downplay the role of emotion, thought, spirit, or other types of human functioning. He simply shows how the body is the substratum or ground for all the activities that go with being a person.

(Notes, ideas, sketches, reactions to the exercises . . .)

*(Notes, ideas,
sketches, reactions
to the exercises . . .)*

_____

_____

_____

_____

_____

_____

_____

_____

_____

_____

_____

_____

_____

_____

_____

_____

_____

_____

_____

_____

_____

_____

*(Notes, ideas,
sketches, reactions
to the exercises . . .)*

Geste

Geste (pronounced "jest") is a concept that occurs frequently, in different forms, throughout modern and contemporary performance theory. Michael Chekhov devised his own version of the concept, which he called "psychological gesture," to help integrate the actor's inner and outer life. Bertholt Brecht used the term *gestus* to describe the movement and positioning of actors in ways that reveal social relationships between characters. Echoes of the concept also occur under various labels in the pedagogy of Copeau, St. Denis, Barrault, Vakhtangov, Meyerhold, Grotowski, and Barba.

My approach to geste is a blend (and an interpretation) of several of these sources, but a blend that points to the broad array of styles and circumstances in which contemporary actors are required to work.

A geste is a pattern of movement that the actor uses to create a fundamental form for the character. The form established by the geste summarizes or symbolizes the character in some way. For example, the geste for a compulsively intrusive person might be a constant pushing of the nose in the direction of everyone and everything he or she meets.

A geste is three-dimensional. Besides helping the actor to create a physical form, it also excites an appropriate psychological life in the actor and leads him or her to the character's social attitudes. That probing nose mentioned in the last paragraph might help the actor discover and express hostility and a superior bearing toward others. Like body centers and body strategies, gestes transform an actor according to the outline supplied by a specific character. But the path to transformation differs from those provided in the last two chapters.

Instead of relying on metaphors like "center" and "strategy" to shape the exercises, gestes depend on metaphors from music and dance. Most of the exercises leading to the discovery of gestic patterns involve rhythmic motion and sound. In fact, another way to describe a geste is as a pattern of movement that captures a character's fundamental rhythm. A geste may be used in several ways. On the one hand, an actor is free to let the character's geste remain obvious in performance. Commedia del l'arte and French boulevard farce are sometimes called gestic styles precisely because they use heightened movements and postures to create character types. In most cases, however, when an actor is not developing a type, a geste becomes a point of departure rather than a result—a method for exploring a character. By the time a play opens, its impact on the actor is supposed to be subtle and unconscious: in the background of his or her performance instead of the foreground. Viewed as a method rather than solely a product, a geste may change over time as the actor learns more about the character and the play.

EXERCISES

Geste I: Text, Music, Rhythm

Working up a geste for your character requires close examination and study. So, at this point, make sure you have a character in mind with which you are familiar. If you are using a scene from the Appendix, make sure you have read the entire play more than once.

Exercise 15–1: Musical Correlatives

1. Choose one to three *short* sections from the play that are particularly helpful in understanding your character.

2. Read them three or four times silently.

3. What kind of music do you associate with your character?

4. Be specific. You may be reading an Elizabethan play but associate your character with do-wop music.

5. Find one or two pieces of music that fit your character in the various beats you've chosen.

6. Read your lines while listening to the music.

7. When possible, sing the dialogue to the melody.

Exercise 15–2: Sound and Rhythm Chant

1. Find a single line that captures something especially important about your character.

2. Try to find a dominant sound pattern that emerges from the line. For example, a line (certainly not the only line) from Eric Overmyer's *On the Verge* that helps me understand Mary comes at the very end of the play, when she says: "I have such a yearning for the future!" For me, Mary's zest for new experience is right at the core of who she is. Here is one sound pattern that emerges from her line: Ay-av-uch-ay-ear-ffffoooor.

3. Say your own sound pattern a few times. Play with it.

4. Chant it in various rhythms for a minute or two until you find one that seems right. How does it make you feel? Upbeat? Down? Mad? Glad?

5. Alternate chanting the sound pattern and saying the entire line. You are under no obligation to transfer the rhythm to the whole line. Relax and let things happen.

Guidelines: To create a vocal rhythm, you have to involve other physical muscle structures. So, rhythmic utterance is one way to connect your voice to the rest of your body.

Exercise 15–3: Sound, Rhythm, Movement

1. Continue chanting your line.

2. Gradually add rhythmic movement. Use as much of your body as possible. Notice how the geste makes you feel. Happy? Angry? Energized? Perhaps your feelings change.

3. After two or three minutes, begin reducing your movement until you are standing still. Then say the entire line in a normal voice two or three times.

Exercise 15–4: Song and Dance with a Partner

1. Do the chant and movement you have just developed in a dialogue with a partner.

2. Your partner's chant and dance need not be from the same play.

3. Continue the dialogue until you can focus on one another and your song and dance are working more or less automatically.

4. Vary the size and speed of your work.

Guidelines: You may be working with a partner who is using lines from a different scene or play. This doesn't matter. In fact, it points up the fact that what you are exchanging is not just intellectual sense (words) but entire physical rhythms.

Exercise 15–5: Back to the Text

1. Resume where you left off with your partner.

2. Gradually reduce the size of your gestes until you are exchanging whole lines in a normal voice.

3. "Forget" your gestes by focusing on one another. What social attitudes do you experience? Servile? Friendly? Powerful? In charge? Do your attitudes change?

Guidelines: Take your time.

Geste II: Through-Line

A particularly effective geste is one built on the through-line of the character you are playing. According to Stanislavski, a through-line, or super-objective, is the infinitive that defines what your character is doing throughout the entire play. For example, Oedipus's through-line might be to find the murderer of Laius; Hamlet's, to revenge the murder of his father or to cleanse Denmark of disease. Willy Loman seems to be trying to win back the love of his son, Biff, or, more broadly, to win back his place as head of the family. The various scene objectives and intentions characters pursue in each beat contribute in some way to the realization of the more general through-line. The following exercises will help you clarify your through-line and personalize it deeply through the work of the body.

Exercise 15–6: From Through-Line to Dance

1. Select a through-line for the character you have chosen. Find a physical gesture that serves to accomplish the through-line or that in some way expresses the infinitive physically. For example, Oedipus's physical gesture might be the motion that goes with looking for clues in obscure places.

2. Repeat the movement until it involves your entire body.

3. Find a rhythm for it. Work for a while allowing the geste to change naturally until it settles and becomes consistent. Notice your feelings.

Exercise 15–7: Geste as Personal Want

1. Recall that intentions can be expressed as statements of personal desire. The same holds true for super-objectives. Begin by transposing your infinitive into a personal desire. For example, Willy Loman's aim to win back the love of his son might become "I want Biff to embrace me."

2. Resume the rhythm you created in the last exercise. Repeat your personal desire out loud in time to your movement. If necessary, change

your movement to fit your personal desire. Maintain your movement pattern for two or three minutes. Notice the emotions that occur. Are they different from those in the last exercise?

3. Reduce the size of your work until you are aware only of saying the line simply and clearly. Let go of the geste (rhythmic movement).

4. Move through the room saying the line to various class members and listening as they say theirs. Become aware of your social attitudes. Do you feel superior or less powerful? Perhaps you simply feel like one of the gang.

Geste III: Central Obstacle

Just as it is frequently useful to find a super-objective that works through an entire play, so too it is possible to discover a central obstacle that seems to define a character's major problem or conflict. Individual obstacles in particular beats are really specific versions of this central obstacle. For example, the central obstacle confronting Oedipus might be the stubborn silence of others. Shepherds, messengers, and the prophet Tiresias all clam up on the subject of Oedipus's childhood. Similarly, if Romeo's through-line is to make Juliet his wife, his central obstacle might be the blood feud between their two families, which helps to generate most of the individual obstacles he encounters throughout the play. An obstacle geste, then, is a movement pattern that helps you develop (1) a deep sensitivity to a character's central obstacle and (2) a desire to overcome it.

Exercise 15–8: From Obstacle to Dance

1. Select an obstacle for your character that summarizes his or her conflict throughout the play.

2. Find a movement which captures that obstacle simply and clearly. For example, if you are playing Romeo, you might imagine yourself as the rope in a tug-of-war, with the Montagues and the Capulets on each side, pulling you back and forth.

3. Do the movement you have decided upon, allowing it to involve your whole body.

4. Let a rhythm set in. Notice what emotions it seems to instill.

Exercise 15–9: No

1. Continue your rhythmic movement, exaggerating until it grows just a bit uncomfortable. (Be careful not to let the discomfort become too extreme.)

2. Begin saying the word *no* to the beat of your motion. Start quietly and build gradually.

3. On the last and loudest "no," break free from your geste.

4. Remain still and loosen for a minute. Notice the feelings, associations, and sensations that occur as you relax.

Exercise 15–10: Including the Text

1. Find a line that captures your character's opposition to his or her central obstacle. For instance, early in the play Romeo says to Juliet: "Thy kinsmen are no stop to me" (II.i.). Some lines are not so direct. (Even Romeo's pronouncement leaves out one-half of his problem—namely, his own kinsmen's contribution to the feud.) You may have to settle for an approximation.

2. Now combine the geste you discovered in the last exercise with the line you have chosen. Incorporate the words into the rhythm of your movement. Exaggerate. Notice what feelings occur as you work.

3. Continue the geste for a minute or two. Then gradually reduce its size until you become unaware of it. Say the line clearly and simply a few times.

4. Move about the room saying your line to others and listening to theirs. Pay attention to what social attitudes arise.

Geste IV: The Neutral Mask

Another path to a character geste is through the use of a neutral mask. A neutral mask is paradoxical. It both conceals and reveals. The mask covers the face but has no expression painted on it (that is why it is called neutral). Therefore, the actor must rely on the rest of his or her body to capture and reveal the character to others. In other words, the actor must compensate for the lack of facial expression. Used in this manner, a neutral mask provides a means of discovering a character's movement, alignment, and voice, which, in turn, help the actor experience an appropriate inner life.

The specific physical pattern taken on by the actor in response to the mask is the actual geste. After the geste has formed, the actor discards the mask, allowing its influence to become unconscious. Of course, the actor can always go back and use the mask to discover new gestes as his or her understanding of the character changes.

For actors like Jean Louis Barrault, who studied with Michel St. Denis, neutral masks lent freedom to the exploration of character by bequeathing a sense of social anonymity on the actor and reducing the pressure to come up with a complete characterization too quickly. Working with a neutral mask is, after all, a process.

The mask, a fixed, yet infinitely variable thing with the power to shape and be shaped, exchanges life-energy with the actor who wears it.

RICHARD ALAN WHITMORE,
THE NEUTRAL ACTOR: FROM COPEAU TO GROTOWSKY, AND BEYOND

Dime stores and novelty shops often have full-face masks without expressions painted on them. These will do just fine. But there are also several ways to make a neutral mask. Perhaps the simplest is to take a brown, paper shopping bag and turn it into an open-ended tube by cutting off the bottom. Then cut holes in one of the sides for your eyes, nose, and mouth. Wear the mask so that the bottom rim of the bag rests on your shoulders. This will keep the holes from sliding out of position. If the bag is too roomy, make a crease along its length directly behind your head. Hold the crease in place with paper clips or a clothes-line pin. (Safety pins are unwieldy and dangerous.)

Exercise 15–11: The Mask as a Projection Screen

1. Set your mask upright in front of you and look at it.

2. Talk to the mask as though it were the character you have chosen to play. Ask it questions and listen carefully to the answers. (You may do this silently or out loud.)

3. Allow it to ask you questions. Answer honestly.

4. Project a look or a specific expression onto the mask. Use your imagination.

Exercise 15–12: Communicating the Face on the Mask

1. Put on the mask and try to transmit the expression that you projected onto it.

2. Since your mask really has no expression on it, you will have to use the rest of your body to communicate what you saw.

3. Explore movement, sound (but not words), and postures that will get a sense of your character across to other members of the class. *Look for a single, simple pattern.* For example, if the expression you saw was happy and upbeat, you might come up with a geste that combines a clownish leap in the air with a glad laugh.

4. As you do this exercise, more questions will probably develop. Have a second conversation with your mask. Repeat the exercise two or three more times. Allow your geste to settle or change.

Guidelines: Repetitions of this exercise are most productive if they are preceded by rereading all or part of the script.

Exercise 15–13: Integrating the Geste

1. Repeat the geste you have discovered until you find a distinct rhythm. Continue the rhythm for two or three minutes.

2. Reduce the size of the movement and sound, gradually coming to a stop.

3. Take off the mask and put it in an upright position again.

4. Talk to it. Let the conversation go where it will. Forget about your geste and let it work subconsciously as you converse.

5. Leave your mask and roam around the room. Improvise short conversations with other students while remaining in character.

Exercise 15–14: Including Others

1. Stand in a circle with classmates.

2. Show them your mask as you introduce your character. Keep your comments brief: one or two sentences.

3. Play music that you think captures some important aspect of your character's mood or personality.

4. As it plays, pass the mask around the room, allowing each person to put it on and come up with a simple geste.

5. When it comes back to you, do your own geste based on what you have assimilated from others.

Exercise 15–15: Inhaling the Mask

1. Prop your mask up in front of you.

2. Breathe freely as you look at it. Wait until your breathing is nice and relaxed; then go on to the next steps.

3. Pause (hold your breath) for two or three seconds at the end of your inhalation. During the pause, try to project a face onto your mask. When an image emerges, exhale and breathe normally. Focus on the details of the face. See the eyes, nose, mouth, chin, etc.

4. Once you can see an expression, imagine you are inhaling it with the air into your lungs. Let it inform your entire being—body, feelings, attitudes, and soul. Take your time. Actually feel the mask enter and begin to transform your body. Put on the mask.

Exercise 15–16: From Posture to Movement

1. Find a simple movement that comes out of the posture you have just discovered. Make the movement rhythmic.

2. After two or three minutes of movement, begin to reduce the size of your work until you are still.

3. After a minute, place your mask where it was at the beginning of the last exercise. Look at it as you go back to a free and natural breathing rhythm.

4. As you breathe, be attuned to whatever inner states arise. You don't have to do anything; just notice them.

5. Wait a minute or two, then get up and move about the class. As you meet others, say one of your character's lines, whichever comes to mind. You can repeat the same line or change it. Let yourself be.

Role Masks

Strictly speaking, a role is not a character. Rather, a role is a social function that a character performs within a play in order to get what he or she wants from others. Lear, for example, is the name of a character. But that character plays a variety of roles, including, among others, pompous king, smartass, benefactor, hell-raiser, victim, and loving father. Some characters play more roles than others. For instance, Lula, in *Dutchman,* spends over half the play functioning as a seductress, whereas Purlie, from *Purlie Victorious,* moves from rebel, to evangelical preacher, to irate father, to rescuer, but not necessarily in that order. Masks and gestes are effective tools in helping an actor clarify and distinguish the various roles his or her character plays in the same production.

Exercise 15–17: Naming the Mask

1. Sit or stand before your mask. Establish an easy breathing rhythm.

2. Now, give your mask a name that captures one of the roles your character plays. Contemporary psychology provides lots of role labels: victim, victimizer, rescuer, mother, father, parent, child, teacher, student, slave, master, and so on. Any label will do as long as it (1) captures the role accurately and (2) awakens your imagination.

3. Pause briefly between inhaling and exhaling. During each pause, imagine a facial expression on the mask that captures the role you have chosen. For example, if you have chosen the role of master, you might project the face and expression of a king.

4. Inhale the expression on the mask into your body. Let it fill you.

5. Put the mask on and begin exploring sounds and movement that will make the role label clear for the rest of the class.

6. Remember again that others cannot see your face. So use the rest of your body.

7. Once you have found a geste that clarifies the role, stop.

Exercise 15–18: Role/Mask/Dialogue

1. Move about the room exchanging your geste with others as a dialogue. Exaggerate and keep the mask on.

2. After three to five minutes, go back to the place you started the last exercise.

3. Be still and remove your mask. Breathe comfortably as you study it. Has the expression changed? Has the role changed or become more specific?

Exercise 15–19: Back to the Text

1. Put your mask back on.

2. Choose a line from your play that goes with the role you have been developing in the previous exercises. Say it several times.

3. Then leave the mask behind and move through the room exchanging your line with others. As you work, let go of your geste, allowing it to become subconscious.

Role masks and the gestes they engender are simple and effective ways of establishing subtle or striking changes in your character as he or she moves from one portion of the play to the next.

Gestes help you make discoveries about your character. But they are also connective. They express feelings and social attitudes that can stimulate your partner. Gestes that create only physical shape without a corresponding inner life are hollow and self-serving: portraiture rather than drama.

Moreover, a geste is a means of personal release. It both stimulates energy and gives it a form by which to influence the world of the play. Appropriate form is what transforms the actor's energy into a powerful and well-defined presence.

REFERENCES

Black, Lendly. *Mikhail Chekhov as Actor, Director, and Teacher.* Ann Arbor, MI: UMI Research Press, 1987. This dissertation spends considerable time clarifying the notion of psychological gesture. It also adds to our knowledge of Chekhov by incorporating information from several new Russian sources.

Brecht, Bertholt. *Little Organum for Theatre.* In *Brecht on Brecht,* edited and translated by John Willett. New York: Hill and Wang, 1964.

Chekhov, Michael. *Lessons for the Professional Actor.* New York: Performing Arts Journal Publications, 1985. The book is a collection of notes taken by Deidre Hurst du Prey in 1941. Chekhov originally taught these fourteen lessons to professional actors who were interested in his work. Comments on psychological gesture are found in Chapters 9–11.

Cole, David. *The Theatrical Event: A Mythos, A Vocabulary, A Perspective.* Middletown, Connecticut: Wesleyan University Press, 1975.

Gordon, Mel. *The Stanislavsky Technique*. New York: Applause Theatre Book Publishers, 1987. Mel Gordon presents lists of exercises beginning with the early pedagogy of Stanislavski through the work of Vakhtangov and Michael Chekhov, and back to the later work of Stanislavski. Chapters 4 and 5 present the important features of Chekhov's system of actor's training.

Whitmore, Richard Alan. "The Neutral Actor: From Copeau to Grotowsky, and Beyond." Ph.D. diss., University of Kansas, 1990. Whitmore's dissertation synthesizes a lot of French sources and adds to our understanding of the place of the neutral mask in modern French acting and pedagogy.

(Notes, ideas, sketches, reactions to the exercises . . .)

*(Notes, ideas,
sketches, reactions
to the exercises . . .)*

_____

_____

_____

_____

_____

_____

_____

_____

_____

_____

_____

_____

_____

_____

_____

_____

_____

_____

_____

(Notes, ideas, sketches, reactions to the exercises . . .)

Theater is situated between all the contending forces that give it life; and theater is itself a life-giver. . . . *Theater is a playing-with-playing. Even the heaviest tragedy has an irreducible kernel/core of the lusory. . . . From Latin* ludus *(a game) and* ludere *(to play). From Old Irish* loid *(a song). Also Middle Irish* laidim *(to exhort or admonish). And Greek* loidoros *(insulting). And Old Celtic* leut *(to be joyous).*

RICHARD SCHECHNER, ENVIRONMENTAL THEATER

Learning to act is not a completely linear journey. In this book, one lesson has to follow another, and, for the sake of precision and depth, acting skills must be presented one at a time. But they must ultimately all mix and work together. The part of the learning process that makes this happen is called assimilation. Assimilation means letting all of the skills become part of you so that they work in a coordinated way. There is no simple formula for making assimilation happen. But there are some practices that can help. Repeating some of the exercises but in a different order (say, repeating Chapter 10 on action and then moving back to Chapter 9 on ways to combine the given circumstances) can create new awarenesses about acting and help skills to blend in different ways. Another approach is to do specific scene work which forces you to use skills that still seem a little out of your reach.

However, assimilation requires more than variations in the exercises and work strategies. The way you connect acting to other parts of life is a major determiner of how you assimilate skills. In other words, you cannot learn to act by focusing only on the exercises. Understanding your own life and the life around you is what allows acting skills to become part of you. To explore acting is to explore yourself in the world. Acting is not self-contained. You must let it connect you to experiences and ideas beyond the greenroom. Discussions of socialization, sensory preference, Whitman's sense of the living environment, masks and social roles, and so on, which occur throughout this book, are attempts on my part to create connections that allow assimilation to happen. If some of the connections I have made between acting and other parts of your life are not satisfying, discover your own. What you do in your performance courses is supposed to activate your humanity on the stage. But what if you have no humanity to activate? We are born primates, but we must work to become human. Live gracefully and learn all that you can.

As Ronald Willis has said,

> I have seen actors who move and speak wonderfully, and who are seemingly full of conviction. But when you look into their eyes, you realize there's no one home.

But there are other actors who have assimilated their training through broad and rich contexts of learning, sensitivity, and awareness—actors for whom acting skills are not just apparatus but integrated means of exploration and expression. To witness their work is to see yourself anew and to get a glimpse of who you are and what you could become.

REFERENCES

Schechner, Richard. *Environmental Theater.* New York: Hawthorn Books, Inc., 1973.

Jumps and Scenes

I have provided several jumps and scenes for use with those exercises that require dialogue.

Jumps are very flexible, short exchanges dealing with general sorts of human situations—in this case, arrivals and departures. The characters are defined in a way that allows them to be played by either men or women and in a variety of circumstances. It usually helps to memorize all the lines in a particular jump so that you can work with anyone in the class at any time.

The scenes are less general and specify particular characters.* But they too are intended to be used in a variety of ways. Most are long enough to be divided into smaller sections, depending on the wishes of your instructor or your own needs. Memorizing a small portion of a scene is usually more convenient when working with the exercises in class. Larger sections may be better for long-term assignments. Most of the stage directions have been removed in order to give you and your instructor the opportunity to determine what sort of surrounding circumstances will be most useful. A lot depends on which chapter you are working on and what your teacher is trying to get across.

Both the jumps and the scenes are intended to help you practice and apply the skills taught in this book. It is important that you do not get hooked on just one way of doing any of them. No single approach is the right one. The overall style of your work should be a by-product of the instructions that go with the various exercises.

---

*I wish to acknowledge the kind work of Robert Leff, the graduate assistant who both helped me select the scenes and then carried out the complex procedures for getting permission to print them.

JUMPS

Arrivals

1.

    A. So, you're back again?

    B. No place else to go. This is where I belong.

    A. You mean this is home?

    B. Yeah, something like that.

2.

    A. You made it. Great to see you.

    B. Thanks. I didn't think I'd get a plane.

    A. How was your flight?

    B. O.K. Crowded. The airport was a mess.

    A. What are you going to do?

    B. As little as possible—for a while. Then I'm going to try and have a normal life for a change.

Departures

3.

    A. Are you leaving?

    B. Yes.

    A. Why?

    B. I've got my reasons.

    A. Can you talk about them?

    B. Not really. I just need something new.

4.

    A. Why are you leaving so soon?

    B. I have lots to do.

    A. There's never enough time.

    B. Look, I wish I could stay. But I can't.

    A. I hope you can come back soon.

    B. So do I.

SCENES

Anton Chekhov, *The Seagull.*

One man and one woman.

TREPLEV: We are alone.

NINA: I think someone is watching.

TREPLEV: No. No one.

NINA: What kind of tree is this?

TREPLEV: It's an elm.

NINA: Why is it so dark?

TREPLEV: Because it's evening. Everything is becoming dark. Please, don't leave early.

NINA: I must.

TREPLEV: What if I go with you. I'll spend the night in your garden and watch your window.

NINA: Please, no. The guard will notice you. And the dog's still not used to you. He'll bark.

TREPLEV: I love you.

NINA: Shhh.

Translated by Samuel G. Marinov, 1990. Adapted by John Gronbeck-Tedesco.

Howard Korder, *Boy's Life.*

One man and one woman.

Don's room. Lisa has found a pair of panties.

LISA: And that's all you have to say about it?

DON: What else do you want me to say?

LISA: How about sorry?

DON: Well, of course I'm sorry. How could I not be sorry?

LISA: You haven't said it.

DON: I'm sorry.

LISA: No you're not. (*Pause.*) I'm going.

DON: Um . . .

LISA: What?

DON: I, ah . . .

LISA: YES? WHAT? WHAT IS IT?

DON: I just think you should realize that I've been under a lot of strain lately.

LISA: I see.

DON: And maybe, I've, you know, handled some things badly—

LISA: You're under a lot of strain so you go off and fuck somebody else.

DON: That's unnecessarily blunt.

LISA: Christ but you're a cheeky bastard. Couldn't you even bother to clean up before I came? Put away the odd pair of panties?

DON: I thought they were yours.

LISA: I don't buy my panties at Job Lot, Don. And I have a low opinion of people who do.

(She throws the panties at him. He fools with them and puts them over his head like a cap.)

DON: They keep your ears warm.

LISA: You think I'm kidding, don't you? You think, well, Lisa's just having a little episode, it'll all blow over, chalk it up to boyish exuberance, hit the sack? Who the fuck do you think you are, James Bond? *(Pause.)* Did you use a condom?

DON: Huh?

LISA: A condom. You know what they are. You see them on TV all the time.

DON: Wha—why?

LISA: Because you slept with her, and then you slept with me, and you don't know who she's been fucking, do you, Don? DO YOU?
(Pause.)
I'm going.

DON: Where?

LISA: I'm going to lie down in traffic, Don. I'm going to let a crosstown bus roll over me because my life is meaningless since you betrayed me. I'm going to my apartment, you stupid shithead!

DON: Lisa, it was just a very casual thing. It's over.

LISA: What do I care?

DON: I made a mistake, I admit that, but . . .

LISA: But what?

DON: It made me realize something, something very important.

LISA: Yes?

DON (*very softly*): I love you.

LISA: What? I can't hear you.

DON: I said I . . .

LISA: I heard what you said! You love me! That doesn't mean shit! This isn't high school, I'm wearing your pin. You want me to tell you what really counts? Out here with the graduates?

DON: What?

LISA: It's not worth it! Do what you want, it doesn't matter to me. I don't even know you Don. After four months I don't know who you are, why you do what you do. You keep getting your dick stuck in things. What is that all about, anyway? Will someone please explain that to me? (*Pause.*) Don't look at me that way.

DON: What way?

LISA: Like a whipped dog. It's just pathetic.

Reprinted by permission of Grove Weidenfeld, a division of Grove Press, Inc. Copyright © 1988 by Howard Korder.

John Olive, *Minnesota Moon.*

Two men.

LARRY: You scared at all?

ALAN: Scared? 'Bout leavin' Maple Lake and goin' up to the big city where I don't know anybody to study at a university with fifty thousand other students where I don't know what I'm gonna study and where I'll live in a dorm with a total stranger who'll be overweight and fart a lot and where I'll be lucky to have enough spending money to buy a pack of Juicy Fruit on Saturday night?

LARRY: Really scared, eh?

ALAN: No.

LARRY: Bullshit.

ALAN: I'm not really. Just kinda numb, layin' back, sayin' "Let's see how the kid handles this one." I ain't scared, just very interested.

LARRY: Well, good luck, Al.

ALAN: Thanks.

(*Pause.*)

LARRY: Been thinkin' 'bout my tax money.

ALAN: Your tax money.

LARRY: Gonna be close to five hundred dollars if I can get some overtime in over Christmas.

ALAN: And you're gonna put it in your car.

LARRY: Damn right. Mags 'n headers.

ALAN: Big tires.

LARRY: Right.

ALAN: Fancy hubcaps.

LARRY: Hubcaps, fuck. I'm talkin' 'bout mags. And chrome headers 'cause I can use the torque wrench at the station.

ALAN: What's a torque wrench?

LARRY: A special kind a' wrench with a gauge that lets you measure how tight you got a bolt in. Sometimes you gotta be careful 'cause if a bolt's too tight, the engine heat'll snap it off or if it's too loose . . . if it's too loose, you could lose oil pressure or the engine'll corrode up on ya.

ALAN: "I can't do anything. I'm stuck in Maple Lake. Ain't got the smarts to go to . . . "

LARRY: Hey.

ALAN: "I can't get the grease off my hands, or the hayseeds outta my hair."

LARRY: I never said . . .

ALAN: Shit.

LARRY: Come on.

ALAN: You know how cars run. You can take 'em apart and fix 'em.

LARRY: Everybody can do that.

ALAN: I can't do it.

LARRY: Well, you're stupid.

ALAN: That's what I'm trying ta tell ya'.

LARRY: Hey, got a new dance step.

ALAN: Cindy taught you?

LARRY: Yeah, watch this. (*Stumbles.*)

ALAN: Drunken fool.

LARRY: Fuck you, I can do it. It's tricky, is all. (*Dancing energetically and singing off key.*)
"Hot time, summer in the city.
Back a' my neck gettin' dirty and gritty.
Cool cat, isn't it a pity,
Gonna dance in every corner of the city."

ALAN: Yeah, alright! You could quit your job at the gas station and become a go-go boy.

LARRY: Remember the dances, Al? (*Alan laughs.*) You 'n me, Terry, Winkie, Jim. What a bunch of rowdies. The time Terry decided he was gonna dance with every girl in the place. Where was that?

ALAN: (*Still laughing.*) I can't remember. Somewhere by Lake Crystal.

LARRY: Five minutes and two fights.

ALAN: You looked real sexy with your fat lip.

LARRY: What a crazy fucker Terry was.

ALAN: Really.

LARRY: With his practical jokes, his runnin'. He had . . . he had . . .

ALAN: Creativity.

LARRY: He had a lotta that, yeah.

ALAN: The most creative person I ever knew. Everything he did, he did his way, his style.

LARRY: (*Counting on his fingers.*) May, June, July . . .

ALAN: Four and a half months.

LARRY: Huh?

ALAN: It's been four and a half months.

LARRY: Since Terry . . . (*Still counting.*) Yeah, right. Four and a half . . . (*After a pause.*) Alan?

ALAN: Yes, Lawrence?

LARRY: Hey, fuck you.

ALAN: What.

LARRY: I sorta wouldn't mind talkin' 'bout Terry. (*Pause. Alan gets up and opens a beer.*) Because I think about him all the time and maybe one a' the reasons I don't know what the fuck I'm doing is because I can't get Terry off my mind.

ALAN: Yeah, yeah, yeah.

LARRY: I mean, it shouldn't take four and a half months to . . .

ALAN: You want one?

LARRY: Huh? No, I got half a' one here. You miss him as much as I do? Al?

ALAN: Whadda ya' think?

LARRY: You pissed?

ALAN: No.

LARRY: Seen his ma lately?

ALAN: Yeah, today. Went over to say good-bye.

LARRY: Yeah? How is she? How's the place look?

ALAN: She's fine, place looks like shit.

LARRY: Nobody around to . . .

ALAN: She's gonna sell it and move up with her daughter.

LARRY: In California?

ALAN: No, the one in Duluth.

LARRY: Oh, yeah. So . . . You said good-bye.

ALAN: Yep.

LARRY: She cry, or anything?

ALAN: Hey.

LARRY: What.

ALAN: You think life's a movie?

LARRY: I dunno what life is.

ALAN: Just somethin' for you to . . .

LARRY: All I asked . . .

ALAN: It was a private . . .

LARRY: (*Overlapping.*) Did she . . . ?

ALAN: . . . conversation! Jesus.

LARRY: Okay, you don't have to tell me. I ain't your friend, I wasn't Terry's friend, I'm just a nosy sonofabitch who can't keep his mouth shut.

ALAN: (*After a pause.*) We talked about Minneapolis, about how hard I would have to study and would I have enough money.

Reprinted by permission of Susan F. Schulman, Inc. Copyright © 1977 by John Olive.

James McLure, *Laundry and Bourbon.*

Two women.

ELIZABETH: God I hate laundry.

HATTIE: Try doing it for three kids.

ELIZABETH: Week in. Week out. It's the same old clothes.

HATTIE: You can only look at so many pairs of Fruit of the Loom before you want to puke.

ELIZABETH: I'd like to burn everything in this basket and start all over. Everything except this shirt.

HATTIE: Why that shirt's all frayed.

ELIZABETH: It is now, but I remember the first time Roy wore this shirt.

HATTIE: When was that?

ELIZABETH: On our first date. He drove up in that pink Thunderbird in this shirt with all the pearl buttons. He looked just like Paul Newman in Hud. (*Hattie holds up a pair of boxer shorts.*)

HATTIE: God these shorts are big.

ELIZABETH: What?

HATTIE: These jockey shorts they're so big. They're not that wide. They're for a narrow body, but they're so long . . .

ELIZABETH: I suppose.

HATTIE: . . . Why're they so long?

ELIZABETH: Roy likes them big. Says he needs a lot of room.

(*Pause.*)

HATTIE: Whew it's hot out here. (*Pause.*) Lordy, how's a body supposed to keep cool?

ELIZABETH: Nothing to do but fix a bourbon and coke and just sit and sweat.

HATTIE: I can't do that.

ELIZABETH: You can't sweat?

HATTIE: No. Fix a drink in the afternoon in front of the kids.

ELIZABETH: Why not?

HATTIE: Children learn by example.

ELIZABETH: So?

HATTIE: Well, all I need is to come home to a house full of kids sitting around drinking margueritas. You don't know what it's like raising a family.

ELIZABETH: No, I don't.

HATTIE: And lemme tell you, summertime is the worst.

ELIZABETH: What do you do?

HATTIE: I send them outside.

ELIZABETH: In this heat.

HATTIE: I give 'em a salt pill and say, play outside.

ELIZABETH: Don't they collapse from heat prostration?

HATTIE: Anything to slow them down.

ELIZABETH: I wish you'd let me take them sometimes.

HATTIE: Elizabeth you're not used to kids. The strain would kill you. Elizabeth, what are you staring out at the road for?

ELIZABETH: No reason. There's nothing to see.

HATTIE: That's the truth. Nothing green to look at. God, it's depressing living on the edge of a desert.

ELIZABETH: But just think millions of years ago all this land was under water.

HATTIE: Well . . . at least it would have been cool.

ELIZABETH: I like this land, but sometimes it gets too hot and burnt for people. It's still too wild and hard for anything to grow. (*Pause.*) Oh, look Hattie!

HATTIE: What is it?

ELIZABETH: Look at that cloud.

HATTIE: It's just a cloud.

ELIZABETH: Yeah, but look how it's throwing a shadow across the land. God, doesn't that shadow look peaceful gliding over the land. Doesn't it look cool? It reminds me of a cool dark hand stroking a hot surface. (*Pause.*) Lately I've felt so hot and hollow inside I've wanted something to come along and touch me like that.

HATTIE: Elizabeth, what's the matter with you?

ELIZABETH: Nothing, Hattie, nothing.

HATTIE: (*Pause.*) You're doing it again, staring out at that hill. There ain't nothing out there but the highway and the road up to the house. Now, what're you expecting to see?

ELIZABETH: I was hoping to see a 1959 pink Thunderbird convertible come over that hill.

HATTIE: You've got tears in your eyes! Don't you tell me nothing's the matter! What is it? (*Pause.*)

ELIZABETH: Roy's been gone two days. (*Silence.*)

HATTIE: Why that son of a bitch! No wonder you've been so weird. Here, you sit yourself down here. I'm gonna fix you a drink and you're gonna tell me all about it.

ELIZABETH: I don't want another drink.

HATTIE: Hush up. Hattie's taking care of you now. The doctor is in. (*Elizabeth sits. Hattie exits to kitchen, talking.*) I knew there was something wrong the minute I laid eyes on you. First you didn't answer the doorbell, and as soon as I saw you I could tell something was the matter. That son of a bitch. (*Hattie returns, having mixed drinks in record time.*) Well, what brought it on this time?

ELIZABETH: I don't know. Things haven't been the same since he came back.

HATTIE: From Vietnam?

ELIZABETH: Yeah.

HATTIE: I know. I seen the change. But believe me you've been perfect about it.

ELIZABETH: I haven't been anything. I haven't done anything. He was the one that went off for two years. He was the one got shot up. He's the one that has nightmares.

HATTIE: Nightmares.

ELIZABETH: Yeah, almost every night. (*Pause.*) Anyway, now he's back and he can't seem to get nothing started. He made me quit the job at the pharmacy. He worked some out at his Dad's place. He's done some rough-necking out in the oil fields. But then always gets in fights and gets himself fired.

HATTIE: Well . . . what's he got to say for himself?

ELIZABETH: He says he's looking for something.

HATTIE: Hmmmm. What?

ELIZABETH: He doesn't know what. He says everything has changed here in Maynard.

HATTIE: Nothing's changed in Maynard since the Civil War.

ELIZABETH: I want him back the way it used to be.

HATTIE: Elizabeth, he's always been wild and unmanageable.

ELIZABETH: (*Flaring.*) I don't want to manage him. I don't want to break his spirit. That's why I married him, his spirit. Roy Caulder wasn't going to take no crap from anyone or anything. He and Wayne Wilder were gonna shake up the world.

HATTIE: Need I remind you that Wayne Wilder is currently serving five to ten for car theft?

Index